ENGAGE

ENGAGE

Building Your Church
Based Ministry to Men

Iron Sharpens Iron

**IRON
SHARPENS
IRON**

Designed by Dee Dee Heathman

Library of Congress Cataloging-in-Publication data

Doyle, Brian; Stewart, Brad; Fraser Ron F.; Cheshire, Tom; and Enslow, Dave
Engage: Building Your Church Based Ministry to Men
p. cm.
ISBN-13: 978-1-6133-98852 (pbk.)
LCCN: 206918304

First Edition
Printed in the United States of America

To contact Iron Sharpens Iron go to: www.IronSharpensIron.net For further information contact Made for Success Publishing, +1 425 526 6480 or email at Service@madeforsuccess.net.

Contents

ACKNOWLEDGEMENT

The author team of this book agrees that Jesus Christ is the source of life and that has been true for each one of us. It is this fact that compels us to invest into other men and come alongside local churches to help them reach and ENGAGE men.

We believe in the local church. It is God's Design, and our commitment is to help pastors and local church leaders shepherd God's Flock that is under their care. (I Peter 5). This book is the fruit of that conviction and thus is written for church leadership. We know and understand that although this book is about the unique opportunity and privilege of ministry to men, it is also about the man's family and church and community. This is the foundation of our Ministry Philosophy'.

DEDICATION

Each man on the author team wants to dedicate this book to the people who have made it possible for us to be in full-time men's ministry. We thank God for our regional teams and the ministry partners that invest in those ministries. We are especially grateful for our wives and children who have supported God's Call on our life these many years.

Thank you!

Ron Fraser, PointMan Ministries
Brad Stewart, Kingdom Warrior
Tom Cheshire, Relevant Practical Ministry for Men
Brian Doyle, Iron Sharpens Iron
Dave Enslow, Next Steps for Men

INTRODUCTION

As a leader, have you ever wondered why effective ministry to men seems so elusive? Have you ever thought to yourself, "I wonder who is doing this well?" Or maybe you have said, "I would like to meet some men who are a little further down the road on this!" Good news, you get all that and more in *ENGAGE*.

Why have a specific ministry to men? We know that men and women are different and so if we are to help men become fully devoted Christ followers then we will need to move away from gender-neutral ministry to one that includes elements designed for ministry to men.

The Bible starts with the book of Genesis, which means "beginning." We have written this book with the "beginning" in mind. It provides the foundations for beginning an effective ministry to men. We have discovered that we lack the strategy to create an effective ministry so we have provided some proven steps that you can use to build your ministry.

One key element is that it requires a team to have an effective ministry to men. You get the key people that make that team up, why they are needed and what their role looks like.

How do we get the men involved? One of the most common questions asked by pastors and men's leaders literally around the world! We answer that with developing entry points for men.

Now that we have gathered the men, how do move them into life-changing relationships? One biblical model is to gather them in small groups? Ironically one way you get men in a small group is by letting them know there is a path to exit the group.

The five authors of *ENGAGE*, have the common passion for assisting the local church in calling men to Christ and engaging them inside the church. They have put pen to paper to help pastors and leaders develop an effective and sustainable ministry to men. To God be the Glory!

Because each of the five authors is "engaged" in what they share, each chapter is full of practical application, not just book "theory." *ENGAGE* explains in everyday language, how to have an effective ministry to men in the context of your local church.

CHAPTER
1

Vision for Ministry to Men and Through Men

By Ron Fraser

I want to start this chapter by asking, "Where are the men?" Where are the men who are spiritually alive—who have a fire in their bellies, a passion to grow toward God, a passion to grow as men, and a passion or growing toward other men? Where are the men who are willing to take bold risks in their faith, who will live out their faith through active involvement in the Christian community and active outreach to those outside the church community? Despite the fact that men dominate the pastoral staffs of most churches, a masculine vacuum exists within the church today. Men may attend services but tend to stay on the periphery, not really having the heart and passion for actively ministering to others. Lacking a feeling of connection to God and their church, most men feel inadequate to be the spiritual leaders they know they should be. Many men would rather abandon the church, either physically or emotionally, than deal with these feelings of inadequacy.

The Bible tells us that as Christian men and the spiritual heads of our homes we are called to do the following:

- Honor Jesus Christ through prayer, worship, and obedience to his word through the power of the Holy Spirit.
- Practice spiritual, moral, ethical and sexual purity.
- Build strong marriages and families through love, protection, and Biblical values.
- Influence our world by being obedient to the great commandment in Mark 12:30-31 which commands us to love God with all our hearts, with all our minds, with all our souls, and with all our strength, and to love our neighbor as we love ourselves. We as men are also called to fulfill the great commission. It is important to understand that we cannot do one without the other.

The question we need to ask ourselves is, "How can we keep these commitments?" The answer is that we must totally surrender our lives to Christ as our Savior, develop a servant's attitude modeled after that of Jesus Christ, and be a reader, hearer, and doer of God's Word. For a man to keep the commitments listed above, he must pursue vital, trusting relationships with other Christian men, understanding that we need brothers to help us keep our Christian commitments. He must also participate in a Christ-centered, disciple-making ministry to men in his church. Although each and every point I have mentioned is important, allow me to focus and expand on the last one.

I am sure some of you are asking why a man must be involved in a ministry to men and why do you not call it men's ministry?

The answer is that "men's ministry" refers to and involves being in some type of program which is provided for a man's involvement, whereas a "ministry to men" refers to our ability to impact the lives of men as a natural consequence of our walk with God. Therefore, I think it is important that we clarify what is meant by the word "ministry," as it relates to men.

We must recognize how the world has negatively impacted and influenced most men and to understand our unique Biblical role as godly men in an ungodly world. We must know what God's Word says about who we are, what we are to become, and what we are to do.

In recent years, many men have seemingly lost interest in church. These men are not necessarily opposed to going to church; they just do not see the church as being "male friendly" and relevant to them and their needs. Because of this, most men in our communities are spiritually detached. With no spiritual compass, they are in bondage to debt, trapped by pornography, and caught up in numerous addictions and sinful lifestyles. Men are confused about masculinity and are disillusioned by the false promises of wealth and power. Many men have rejected their marriage commitment, and as a result, families are fragmented and falling apart.

all true

Although called by God to be the spiritual leaders, most men are spiritually adrift. Fortunately, a number of pastors and men's ministry leaders see this as a major crisis and are recognizing the great need for their churches to reach out to men. However, most do not know how.

In this chapter, we will try to help you understand what ministry to men and through men looks like, both visible and invisible, and how it must be done in a masculine context that men can relate to and understand.

Ministry to Men and Through Men

I want to begin by explaining what it means to have a vision for ministry to men and through men, and why we need to have such a ministry.

Benjamin Franklin made this statement: "By failing to prepare, you are preparing to fail." A similar statement is made in Proverbs 29:18 (KJV) which says, "Where there is no vision, the people perish." To successfully minister to men, a church must have a clear focus on their goals for ministry or the men will be confused about what they are working toward. One way a clear focus can be developed and maintained is with a clear vision statement or purpose statement. Remember, a vision statement will allow you to develop a well-balanced ministry that includes a system of checks and balances that will tell you how well you are doing in reaching the men of your church and community. One of the toughest jobs leaders face is communicating their vision to their men. Communication needs to be a repetitive process when it comes to men. Consistency, simplicity, and repetition are all very important when you're trying to communicate your vision.

Why Ministry to Men?

So why have a specific ministry to men? To answer this question, we must understand some important needs men have.

First of all, men want their lives to be productive and to have meaning. Men want to be successful and feel significant. Men want to be good husbands, good fathers, and the spiritual leaders of their families. The problem is that many of them do not know how to accomplish these goals.

Many Christian men are not satisfied with their marriage and family lives. They experience stress on the job, they struggle with sexual matters, and they lack relationships with other men with whom they can be open and honest.

The bad news is that the programs the church has used to reach lost men and meet the needs of redeemed men are not sufficient. The good news is that a properly run, properly focused men's ministry can provide the spiritual direction men need to join God's work in every area of their lives. Let me remind you again that a ministry to men that will draw men to Christ, mobilizing them for ministry, must be based on a thorough knowledge of a man's specific needs and characteristics.

Secondly, men represent a tremendous, untapped resource that can have a great impact in changing and influencing our world for Christ.

Despite the very troubling times we are experiencing all around us, there is still a great spiritual hunger that exists in our world today. Over the course of history, we have seen and witnessed various significant life-changing movements in and through men. It might be more correct to say, rather than a movement of men, it is a movement of God's Spirit in and through the hearts of men. The movement, or working of God's Spirit, has little to do with any given men's ministry and has everything to do with God's Sovereignty. This work points to a deep spiritual hunger. Men are discovering that they have a tremendous God-shaped void in their lives that only He can fill. Again, they want their lives to count for something that really will make a difference. Men want their lives to be productive, meaningful and have a genuine purpose.

While doing ministry, if we recognize that God has given men a tremendous, untapped resource that can have a great impact in changing and influencing our world, cities, workplaces, families, neighborhoods, and relationships for Christ, then we will also understand the importance of having an intentional, focused ministry to men.

Henry Varley wrote, "The world has yet to see what God can do with, and for, and through, and in a man who was fully and holy consecrated to Him."

Thirdly, the reason we have a ministry to men is the fact that men are strategic. I am reminded of something Steve Sonderman said: "If ever there was a time in history when local churches needed to build men individually and corporately, it is now." This is especially true as our world deteriorates. Men desperately need and are looking for, a ministry uniquely designed to reach them as men and help them to be the men and leaders God designed them to be. They need a ministry that is focused on the issues they deal with in their everyday lives impacts their walk with God.

It is a given fact that if you reach the men, you will reach the families. Numerous statistics show the importance of churches becoming more intentional in their development of a ministry to men that will attract and grow men for Christ. But, to reach the men, you have to understand their condition and their issues, intentionally enter into their world and specifically address their needs.

The Needs of Men Today

So, what are the needs of men today and where has the church dropped the ball when it comes to ministering to men?

One area they have failed to recognize is that having a focused and intentional ministry to men helps to reach men who have been unreached through the church's other ministries. Men who have rejected traditional ministries and ministry approaches may be more willing to become involved in an athletic program, a "men-only" ministry project, or a mission trip. They do so because of what we will call a masculine context. The male context provides an atmosphere to address male life-issues that cannot be addressed effectively in a mixed or coed environment. Alexander Mitserlich wrote, "Society has torn the soul of the male, and into this tear, the demons have fled—the demons of insecurity, selfishness, and of despair. Consequently, men do not know who they are as men. Rather, they define themselves by what they do, who they know, or by what they own." A man's self-identity is wrapped up almost entirely in what he does. His career gives him a sense of self-worth and defines the kind of man he sees himself as being. Society embraces the self-made individual. The very structure of our society and economy rips a man from his family and tells him that fulfillment is found outside the home.

Men are struggling to find churches that understand them and what life is doing to them. They are looking for meaningful relationships because most men feel lonely, isolated, and disconnected. They want to be connected with like-minded peers in a non-threatening environment. Men need other men to serve them in relationship, yet they are afraid to open up and get close enough for someone to see their needs and how they might be served.

It is important for us to realize that many unchurched men have given up on organized religion but not on God. They want to know God but don't know how.

Men are spiritually lost, caught in cycles of pain, addiction, sin, and more than anything; they are confused about masculinity.

We will take a deeper look at this later in the chapter, but before we do, it is important for us to look at what an effective ministry to men might look like. There have been numerous articles written on the subject from a multitude of vantage points, all coming in essence, to the same conclusion; so, I am not going to try to reinvent the wheel. However, I will highlight what I consider the most important characteristics of a ministry to men.

What an Effective Ministry to Men Looks Like?

It is my belief that to effectively reach men, you must have a ministry to men that has the five following characteristics.

1. It will be Christ-centered with its top priority being listening to and obeying God. An effective ministry to men understands that it is God who does the work in the hearts and lives of men. In an effective ministry to men, you view the ministry as a partnership with God. Before a man can change his ways, he must first change his heart, and only God can change a man's heart.

2. It is prayer driven. For a ministry to move forward and bear lasting fruit, it must move forward on its knees. S.D. Gordon stated, "You can do more than pray after you have prayed, but you cannot do more than pray until you have prayed." Too often prayer becomes the last resort in our efforts to do ministry. We get the mindset that when all else fails—pray. The foundation that is laid for every ministry to men must first begin with a season of prayer.

3. It must be purpose driven. Without a clear and concise purpose, it will be very difficult for a ministry to stay on track.

Hopefully, your end purpose is to make disciples that will, in turn, make disciples. It is not uncommon to find ministries that are doing the right things but do not have direction or focus. Due to this, their ministry to men begins to falter because they are unclear about the ultimate purpose behind what they are trying to do.

4. It must be intentional in the way it does ministry. Remember, your ministry strategy will take you to your purpose. You will need to structure your ministry in a way that will accomplish your mission. There must be bridges built between each event or outreach that you do, bridges that continue to lead men to the "next step" in their discipleship process. Never do an event for the sake of doing an event. Always create a bridge to something deeper.

5. It must be actively supported by the pastor since everything in a church comes from the top down. It has been stated that of all the churches who are effectively ministering to men, 91% traced the success, at least in part, to the support, release, and encouragement from a staff pastor. When a pastor is actively supportive of a ministry to men, the ministry has greater momentum, a stronger foundation, and more readily draws men together. It bolsters a ministry to men when the pastor consistently supports the ministry from the pulpit. Moreover, if he is also in some accountable relationships with other men and shares his experiences with them, then they are even more apt to make commitments themselves. Simply put, men are more likely to do what the pastor does and not what he says. Men are looking for a leader to follow. The only way that a ministry to men can be effective is when the pastor recognizes

the importance of such a ministry, both for the men, and for his church, and supports it wholeheartedly.

Equipping Men for Ministry

When we talk about ministry to men, we must also discuss the idea of ministry through men. Nothing is more exciting than helping men come to God and experience what it is like to have a personal relationship with Jesus Christ. Nothing is more encouraging than helping men grow in Christ as fully devoted followers of Him. In addition, nothing is more empowering than helping men serve in and through their church in ways that match their God-given gifts, abilities, personalities, and life experiences. However, it is common to find men whose growth has been stunted because no one has helped them discover the unique way God has made them and how that relates with what God would have them do in ministry to others.

So, where does a good ministry to men begin equipping men for missional ministry? You begin by helping each man discover their unique make-up for ministry and provide opportunities for them to identify their spiritual gifts. Once you have identified where they might be gifted, match them with a ministry where they can use these gifts to minister to the needs of others. Yes, I know that some differ in the philosophy of how a person identifies his or her gifts. My intent here is not to define how a man becomes aware of his giftedness, but rather my point is that a good ministry to men will help his search to understand the gift(s) that God has given him and to encourage and train him as he serves. By doing this, you are not only doing ministry to men, but you are also doing missional ministry through men.

What Men Are Looking for and Needing in a Church

Earlier in this chapter, we stated that men are spiritually lost, caught in cycles of pain, addiction, and sin. More than anything, they are confused about their masculinity. It is important to note that we are not just referring to men outside the church but also men inside the church who attend on a regular basis.

As we continue to look at the importance of ministry to men, we must take a hard look at the masculine makeup of a man and what he is looking for in a church or ministry. There are a number of qualities men look for in a church; however, I would like to look at the three most important.

1. Men want a church that helps them truly understand the Bible, and they want to know how the church is relevant to the needs they have. They have questions dealing with how they can be better leaders in their homes, church, workplace, and world. The problem is that the church is not speaking to the issues of men, and especially to the needs of the Millennials. Most language in church is very feminine, and the topics of most sermons are not masculine in context.

    I recently read an article by a young female Millennial in which she discussed why she wanted to leave the church. What surprised me was not her reasoning for wanting to leave, but the observation she made about the church in relationship to men. She said that there is a lack of single men in the church today, which she attributed, in part, to a larger issue of males drifting away from "feminized" worship experiences on Sunday mornings. She went on to share that she told a friend that if the church did not change their way of ministering and become less attractional in their style, they would start losing the women as well. The fact that as a young woman she recognized what is happening with men when most pastors have not is very disconcerting to me.

Part of the problem is that in many cases, we are still giving men the milk of the Word when they need to be getting the meat. That was the problem in the church at Corinth that Paul referred to in I Corinthians 3:2.

Men are staggered by the pressures they carry. Most men require that the church provides practical, tangible solutions to the difficult problems they face daily. They want to know spiritual principles that will make life "work" for them. The church must answer the questions men are asking by pointing them back to God's word. The primary goal of an effective ministry to men is to strategically help men transfer biblical truth into action by providing the necessary environments for them to mature in their walk with God and to disciple their families.

2. Men are looking to be challenged. Men view everything around them as something to be conquered. If you ask them what they are sick and tired of, it would be just meeting, eating, and talking. We have to raise the bar with men. Men need to be challenged in their Christian life, in discipleship, and in relationships. Challenges are important in a man's life even though they can bring out the worst in a man. They can be a litmus test when it comes to revealing if he is a fan or follower in his walk with God. Remember, when Jesus challenged the disciples, many of them left. Those who really had the heart for God stayed and became true followers of Christ. Men

want to be part of something bigger than themselves and a solid ministry to men will provide this challenge.

3. Men are looking for a cause, something to work towards that is not easily accomplished. As stated above, it is the true nature of a man to want to be part of something greater than himself. Men are practical creatures. They are doers and task driven. But, that does not mean that they grow by reading only concepts and principles. They need to be inspired. When the book *Wild at Heart* came out, it sold millions. Why? It inspired men. Men want a cause to fight for, something to conquer, and they want to be part of a team to do it.

In an effective ministry to men, it is important to keep the "mission" before them at all times. Men are hungering to be part of a team. A church needs to provide a wide variety of ministries that will challenge and stretch their men. Missional ministry gives a man an opportunity to do activities he does best—problem solve, organize, lead, teach, and build. Not only does the work accomplish something, but the nature of the work is fulfilling and a practical way to use the gifts that God has given them. This can include mission projects, short-term work projects, or anything that allows them to work side-by-side with other men. Remember, in the midst of doing side by side activity, men get saved.

Think about it. Have you ever met a man who woke up in the morning hoping to be a failure? No, they want to succeed. Too often, when a church ministers to men, they fail to give them a vision of manhood. Men need a cause, and they need to be encouraged to be champions of that cause. Champions in life.

Ministry to Men: Visible and Invisible

The last thing we need to look at in this chapter is the idea of visible and invisible ministry to men.

Howard Hendricks, a former professor at Dallas Theological Seminary, said, "Our risen Christ left this legacy—the Magna Carta of the church—to make disciples. He provided both the model and the method. His life and death recast the lives of men. He demonstrated that you have not anything until you have changed the lives of men."

When the church decides to do ministry to men, its success or failure will be determined by the ability it has to develop a balanced ministry plan. It is easy to grow a ministry that gets so caught up in one Biblical mandate that it ignores the others. It is possible, for example, to pour a great deal of energy, money, and time into bringing lost men to Christ, but then spend very little time grounding them in the basics and helping them mature in Christ. On the reverse side of the coin, it is also possible to spend so much time perfecting what you do to mature your men that you never reach out to those outside the faith. That is why a balanced ministry is so important.

Two types of ministry take place when you are ministering to men. There is the visible ministry we do for men and the invisible ministry that is done with men. Notice, I use the words "for" and "with" in my sentence. There is a distinct difference between these two ministries.

A visible ministry for men is done when a church provides opportunities for men to attend conferences, receive training, and participate in support groups, spiritual growth retreats, and bible studies. Most churches that do ministry to men have various approaches to help their men grow in Christ. All of these ministry opportunities are good for helping men find community and build relationships. However, as you establish the purpose of a ministry and begin planning men's activities such as these, it is important to keep a focus on your obedience to God. Through your relationship with God, He will reveal His plans and purposes for your ministry.

An invisible ministry to men is the ministry we do on a daily basis that impacts the lives of men but is not necessarily seen by others. Ministry to men is not just about the big event and visible things that happen with men, it is about things you do not always see. This involves discipling men to spiritual maturity. A foundational aspect of any ministry to men should be that every man is active in building caring relationships with other men, helping them to mature in their walk with God as well as leading them to Christ. It involves one-on-one ministry and creating an atmosphere of accountability, while growing Godly servant leaders in their homes, work, church, and community.

God wants the church to reach men with the gospel of Christ and to help them grow to maturity. The goal here is for men to disciple men who in turn disciple other men. They are to live out the great commandment and to fulfill the great commission in every aspect of their lives—personal, home, workplace, community, and the world. John Maxwell said, "People don't care how much you know until they know how much you care." So how does an effective ministry provide a caring relationship for men? We need to help men build lasting relationships with other men with whom they can have a sense of accountability and trust by providing opportunities for them to develop community.

If you want to see a vibrant ministry to men in your church, you cannot overlook the most essential ingredient of success: vital relationships. You can follow every guideline given in this book, but if you neglect vital relationship building among your men, you will never see an effective ministry to men grow in your church. Remember, ministry to men is all about building intentional and lasting relationships. Unless a man is willing to live like a disciple, he will never have the courage to fully hand over the reins of his career and life to God and cast aside the middle-class values that permeate our culture and suburban churches.

The intent of this chapter has been to show the importance of having a ministry to men and to make each of us aware that a ministry like this does not happen by accident. It has to be an intentional part of our church planning process, and it must be relevant to the men God has called us to serve. We live in a morally corrupt world that has a growing urgency for men to learn to love God with all their hearts, souls, minds, and strength. I have found that in almost every church, there are men longing to grow spiritually, but the pathway for that development is missing.

Some churches have focused so much on including everyone in every church program and event that the spiritual maturity of the church has become anemic. If a church fails to recognize the strategic importance of men and they choose not to be intentional in helping men find answers to the issues they are struggling with, then we will soon see churches closing their doors. Men will have stopped coming because they continue to find that church is not relevant to them. The Millennials are a good example of this in that most are not finding the church to meet their needs.

We understand that the idea of beginning a ministry to men has not always set well with the pastors of many churches. Some have shared with us that it does not fit into their ministry plan. Many churches have implemented more family-centered programs and events in an attempt to help sustain families in the church. Consequently, women have been at the front of this church participation and attention—and the men have taken a back seat. Patrick Arnold in his book, *Wildmen, Warriors, and Kings Masculine Spirituality in the Bible* made this statement, "I hurt inside as I see the great divorce that has developed over the generations between men and Christian Spirituality. I hurt for the men that have lost the close contact with God that a healthy religiosity can nurture. This is an alienation that affects me personally as well as all men."

Healthy churches, on the other hand, have realized the needs of their men and have an intentional focus on discipling men to become leaders in their marriages, families, churches and communities. They have given men the scriptural foundation on which to develop a deeper walk with God. We mentioned the checks and balances of an effective men's ministry. So how do we know if our ministry to men is making a difference? The answer is simple. Ministry to men is not measured by what we pour into a man, but by the fruit that returns from those he pours into.

CHAPTER

2

Beginning a Disciple Making Men's Ministry

By Brad Stewart

A few years back, I was leading a Bible study with three men. To stimulate their thinking, I asked this question: "If you had three months to live, what would you do with your life?" The first individual to speak was single. He said, "I would give away all my possessions and use the money in my bank account to fly to the deepest jungle in Africa to share the gospel with an unreached people group." The second man was married and had a family. He said, "I would do two things. First, I would ensure my home is in order and my immediate family is taken care of. Then, I would sit down and list all my family members who were not saved and create a plan to share the gospel with each one of them." The third man, who was married, said, "I would move my mother-in-law into my home." Stunned by his answer, I asked, "Why would you do that?" He replied, "Because that would be the longest three months of my life."

Granted, this story brings a chuckle, but there is truth to the question and wisdom in the answers. Suppose you had three years to live, what would you do with your remaining time? Jesus faced the same question.

He knew His time on earth was limited. So, what did He do? To find the answer to that question, we need to look at the Gospel of John.

In John 1, we find John the Baptist giving the first real testimony of who Jesus is. After hearing two of John's disciples decided to follow Jesus and seeing them follow Him, Jesus asked, "What do you want?" They replied, "Where are you staying?" Jesus begins His ministry with a few simple but powerful words, "Come and you will see."

Andrew went to Simon, his brother, claiming to have found the Messiah. He brought him to Jesus. The next day Jesus found Phillip and said to him, "Follow me." Phillip found Nathaniel and told him about Jesus. Nathaniel reacted with disbelief. Phillip's answer to Nathaniel is a classic case of mentoring and discipleship. He said, "Come and see."

In the beginning, Jesus surrounded Himself with men. A few months later, He prays all night and selects twelve men to be with Him in ministry together. He knew that an effective disciple-making ministry flows out of men in strong relationships with one another. When it came time to send the disciples out to do the work of the ministry, He sent them out in groups of two and gave them specific training instructions for each mission (Luke 9:1-6; 10:1-17).

In the book of Acts, we see the apostle Paul undertake three missionary journeys (Acts 13:1-4; 15:36-41; 20:4). In each journey, he traveled and worked with a small group of men. Whenever he went into a city to establish a church, the first thing he did was build a ministry team that would carry on after he departed. Toward the end of several New Testament books, we see a list of men and women who worked with Paul to establish new churches and build existing ones (Romans 16:3-15; Ephesians 6:21; Colossians 4:7-17).

While the principles for ministry in these Scriptural chapters are numerous, I want to point out the importance of finding like-minded men who seek truth and desire to make an impact in the world through fulfilling the Great Commission to make disciples of all nations (Matthew 28:18-20).

A.B. Bruce in his classic work, *The Training of the Twelve*, provides this comment on the early ministry of Jesus:

That these calls were given with conscious reference to an ulterior end, even the apostleship, appears from the remarkable terms in which the earliest of them was expressed. "Follow me," said Jesus to the fishermen of Bethsaida, "and I will make you fishers of men." These words (whose originality stamps them as a genuine saying of Jesus) show that the great Founder of the faith desired not only to have disciples, but to have about Him men whom He might train to make disciples of others: to cast the net of divine truth into the sea of the world, and to land on the shores of the divine kingdom a great multitude of believing souls. Both from His words and from His actions we can see that He attached supreme importance to that part of His work which consisted in training the twelve. In the intercessory prayer, e.g., He speaks of the training He had given these men as if it had been the principal part of His own earthly ministry. And such, in one sense, it really was. The careful, painstaking education of the disciples secured that the Teacher's influence on the world should be permanent; that His kingdom should be founded on the rock of deep and indestructible convictions in the minds of the few, not on the shifting sands of superficial evanescent impressions on the minds of the many. Regarding that kingdom, as our Lord Himself has taught us in one of His parables to do, as a thing introduced into the world like a seed cast into the ground and left to grow according to natural laws, we may say that, but for the twelve, the doctrine, the works, and the image of Jesus might have perished from human remembrance, nothing remaining but a vague mythical tradition, of no historical value, and of little practical influence. [1]

Done right and done well, training men in the principles and practices of Jesus should influence others and help your church transform the culture and country in which you live, worship, and serve the Lord.

The rest of this chapter provides you with some key but critical items to consider when starting a disciple-making ministry to and through men. If you complete each section, you will:

- Form a strong foundation based on solid biblical principles that help give you and your men a compelling vision and solid footing.
- Create a reproducible church ministry strategy that captures and sustains momentum.
- Use survey tools to identify the critical needs and wants of your men.
- Develop a three to four-year plan of action with key milestones.
- Conduct event and ongoing ministry activity debrief and evaluate their effectiveness.

Form a Strong Foundation

An effective disciple-making men's ministry needs to focus on a team approach, rather than that of one individual. While one man may have the initial heart, vision, and passion for this ministry, he must develop a team of men around him to change men's lives and achieve the ministry mission successfully. A team allows more men to be involved, use their talents and spiritual gifts, encourage one another, and to accomplish more. Here are several suggested steps for starting a disciple-making men's ministry team.

Work from a Biblical Basis

Men's ministry flows from the great commission which Christ gave His disciples after the resurrection (Matthew 28:18-20). In His final instruction, He provided two main points for going and making disciples of all nations:

- Baptize them in the name of the Father and of the Son and of the Holy Spirit.
- Teach them to obey everything I have commanded you.

Unfortunately, too many churches have abandoned Christ's model of leading by example for a more academic process. Men learn more and follow closer to a living example. Living as an intentional follower of Christ was never intended to be one man imparting knowledge to another. It was intended to be one man helping another walk with God and learn to reproduce life in others. The focus of godly men's ministry is to bring men together and build life into each other through life-on-life discipleship.

Baptizing Men. Baptism is a religious sacrament marked by the symbolic application of water to the head or immersion of the body into water and resulting in the admission of the recipient into the community of Christians. Baptism signifies spiritual cleansing and rebirth. Baptism is a decree of the Lord Jesus Christ for anyone who has repented of their sins and who, by faith, acknowledges the Lordship of Christ, His death on the cross, and His resurrection from the dead. By being covered in water in the name of the Father and the Son and the Holy Spirit, a true believer provides an outward sign of an inward change. He or she now belongs to the new people of God, the true Israel, and plans to go forward living as an intentional follower of Christ and function as a member of His growing kingdom.

There are numerous examples of baptism in the New Testament (Matthew 3:16, Acts 2:38-39, Acts 2:41; 8:12-16; 8:36-38; 9:18; 10:47-48; 16:15-33; 19:3-5; 1Cor. 1:13-16; 15:29; 1Pet. 3:21).

Teaching Them to Obey Christ's Commandments. Christ spent three years imparting His imperatives to His disciples. He expected them to obey His word and to help others understand what it means to obey His word. Today, men are struggling with family, finances, work, sexuality, drugs, and alcohol. If this was not bad enough, some studies show that most men over the age of thirty-five do not have a friend they can call or ask for help. An effective men's ministry should help provide solutions to all of these issues by teaching men to obey the commandments of Christ.

Life-to-life discipleship training helps men focus on areas that are specific to the unique struggles men face. The kind of training that makes men into mature disciples is the kind that helps men with obedience to the Scriptures. There are many great tools to help local churches make disciples. For a list of free tools and job aids, visit Kingdom Warrior's tool site at www.kingdomwarrior.net.

Select Your Men

The first thing you need to do is identify several men who have a passion and heart to join you in your journey.

1. *Pray, pray, and pray some more.* Develop a list of men in your church who you would like to pray with you. Ask them if they would like to meet and pray for men and the men's ministry (Luke 6:12-13; Matthew 18:19-20; 9:36-39). Pray that God would bring the right man into the right position based on his gifts, talents, and availability.

2. *Secure the pastor's approval.* Most pastors would like to know what is going on in their church, even if they do not have time to be active in every type of ministry. Some pastors will make themselves available for men's ministry while others may feel burdened by one more thing to focus on. Don't give up on gaining an active support from your pastor. If he has many concerns, start out small and build from there. Be willing to labor for the kingdom.

3. *Fish for men.* Make contacts through evangelism, Bible studies, prayer meetings, worship, conferences, cell groups, and fellowship meetings. Share your passion for men's ministry and love for God's Word. Look for men who respond with a kindred spirit (Mark 3:13).

4. *Develop a broad base of relationships.* Get to know all the men in your small groups and meet with as many as possible one-on-one. Ministry happens best through existing relationships. Half of Christ's first band of men contained three sets of brothers.

5. *Seek men with different gifts.* It is very natural for a leader to surround himself with men that look, act, and think as he does. Men that we want to become our friends. This can create a big hole in a team's effectiveness. A leader of men needs to surround himself with other men who complement his giftedness. Consider the following motivational gifts based on Romans 12: prophecy, giving/sharing, service, administration, teaching, mercy/helps, and exhortation.

Once you have at least one or two other men who want to see God create a disciple-making men's ministry in your local church, you are ready to create the mission, vision, and guiding principles.

Develop a Mission, Vision, and Set of Guiding Principles

With a few men committed to forming a men's ministry team, you are now ready to build the ministry. Over the course of the first year or two, it is important for the men to develop as a team that facilitates teamwork. They must begin the process of ministering together.

Teams develop as men commit to being a part of the men's ministry team. The men's ministry team must have a clear vision and mission statement to help it stay on course and accomplish the ministry goals. Most men long for an opportunity to be a part of something bigger than themselves. If they are going to sacrifice their time with family and career, invest emotional energy, and physical resources, they want to know it's worth the time, effort, and cost. To maintain forward momentum, leaders must routinely keep the vision, mission, and goals clearly in front of the team.

If you do not already have a vision and mission statement, you need to develop them. There is a saying, "Aim at nothing and you will hit it every time." Having a focused direction is important. A purpose statement provides direction and forms the basis for all of the ministry activities, goals, and guiding principles. Some leaders write an end-state statement that is similar to missions and vision. This can provide added guidance to the team members without a team leader. It also helps the leader begin with the end in mind.

Vision is the biblical mandate for ministry. It is the over-arching reason for doing ministry. The vision statement is usually the broader term and serves as the ultimate ministry fulfillment. Examples:

- Helping men find their way (Steve Farrar)

- Serving the Lord at home, at work, and in the Church (Joshua's Men)
- Advancing the Kingdom of Heaven through the local church (Kingdom Warrior)

Mission helps bring into view some of the specifics of what an organization believes God has called them to do. The mission statement should compel the organization's core leadership team and excite the men in the organization's ministry. In other words, it should motivate! Examples:

- Deepen a man's personal walk with God, develop a man's brotherhood with other men, and disciple a man's life for works of service (Joshua's Men).
- Through the brotherhood of Christ, we strive to help men serve God by using their time, talents, and treasures in an effort to transform their homes, their communities, and their churches for the glory of God. Kingdom Warrior accomplishes this mission by providing excellent men's ministry conferences, workshops, seminars, resources, coaching, and training services to help churches implement an ongoing ministry to and through men (Kingdom Warrior).

Guiding principles are a set of statements that provide personal or group rules of conduct and management. Examples:

- Cultivate a male friendly environment
- Provide opportunities for men to interact
- Teach practical application of the Bible
- Disciple men as intentional followers of Jesus Christ
- Equip men for works of ministry

Together, these form a set of purpose statements. Having a clear purpose statement is critical to keeping men's ministry focused and carrying out the mission. Without focus, a ministry can exist, but never accomplish something significant toward building the kingdom of God. Building the kingdom of God is accomplished by training men to labor in the harvest fields of men's souls. Jesus worked to train His men to enter the harvest fields and fulfill the great commission.

Here are several questions to help you form your vision, mission, and guiding principles. If you feel stuck, look at the definitions above and then examine the samples with each definition. This exercise is best done in a group setting where members brainstorm answers.

Q: What is your vision statement?

Q: What is your mission statement?

Q: What are your guiding principles?

Assess the Church Situation

While there are similarities between local churches, there are also major differences. The following sets of principles are suggestions. Each church and each set of men are unique. It is important to gain knowledge about men and their short and long-term needs with family, church, work, and then develop a plan that targets the need and fulfills the great commission.

Adopt a Sustainable Discipleship Strategy

Effective men's ministries strategically organize different types of gatherings that work together as a whole. The funnel model illustrates how they fit with each other. There are six distinct types of entry points for men: special events, men's conferences, training seminars, congregational meetings, small group meetings, and man-to-man sessions.

FIGURE 1 - THE FUNNEL MODEL

When your men's ministry provides a variety of entry points, you make it easier for men to get involved. The men in your church are in different seasons of life and have different interests. How much they get involved will depend on their interest in spiritual things, their readiness, the time they have available, and whether or not they see value in what is offered.

Another important consideration is the goal for your entry points. Each point should provide an opportunity for men to grow in their relationships with other men. Some events will seem more appealing than others will. One thing you want to avoid is an event or ministry activity that makes a man feel bored or irrelevant. For example, if all the songs listed for a church service are more appealing to women than to men, a lot of men will feel like they don't belong. Another example would be an event that targets women and children. Unfortunately, during these kinds of services, the average guy in church starts to feel irrelevant. Repeatedly, men's surveys rank these as the biggest reasons why men dislike going to church. Each of the following entry points has implications for your church.

Men's Special Events.

Men's special events are strategically designed to be a non-threatening environment for men, especially for men outside the church. Most men in and out of the local church prefer events such as sporting activities, hunting, and fishing. In other words, these events do not make a guy feel like he is in church. It is much easier to get a non-Christian to attend a non-threatening type of event than one specifically designed for men *in* church. These activity-oriented events also offer opportunities for men to become acquainted with each other. Examples:

- Outdoor events
- Recreational events
- Sporting events

Implications: Special events are a great place for men to bring un-churched friends, new men in the church, or those not yet involved.

For a significant amount of your men, this will be the first point of contact with other men in the church. Men at these events communicate on the level of "what they do" and begin to interact with others based on what they have in common. Often, special events provide an opportunity for a man to move from spectator to participant.

Special events are critical first steps for men who need a non-threatening experience where other men will not ask them to do something for which they are not prepared or at that point willing to make. For example, this is not the kind of event to ask a guy to break into a small group or share a personal struggle. Guys on the fringes of your church or in the community are more likely to attend a special event.

Men's Conferences

Men's conferences are an excellent type of event for the local church. These kinds of events act as a catalyst to motivate men and help light a fire to get things going. Use this kind of event to jump-start your ministry to men. Examples:

- Iron Sharpens Iron
- God Men
- Promise Keepers

Implications: Many of the men who attend a male-only regional conference return from these events having made a life-changing commitment to serve Jesus Christ, their families, friends, and their local church.

When the local church captures the momentum from a men's conference, it strengthens the churches mission, families, and leadership. After men return from a regional conference, local men's ministry has a perfect opportunity to capitalize on the spiritual momentum by offering entry points right away into men's small groups, monthly men's breakfast, or other activities.

Men's Training Seminars

Men's ministry workshops, equipping study guides, and training seminars offer men the opportunities to develop in areas specific to being a Christian man. God calls all of His men to grow in their leadership roles. Men who have developed a friendship through a special event or men's conference are more likely to accept an invitation to attend training or equipping seminars. He will have already experienced some sort of event with men whom he can carpool, laugh, or share something about his personal life. Additionally, focused training is an excellent opportunity for a local church to invest in their men's personal growth, ministry vision, and leadership skills. Examples:

- Men's Ministry Leadership
- Fathering
- Evangelism and Discipleship

Implications: In addition to serving as a good entry point, a seminar provides encouragement, practical tools, and training not always available at a regular worship service.

Men's Congregational Events

Men's congregational gatherings provide events where your men can meet for practical teaching from Scripture, fellowship, and prayer. Men's only congregational meeting should have a masculine context that helps men with practical teaching from the Bible, specifically as it relates to male issues. This kind of event helps men develop relationships with other men and deepen their relationship with God. Men start to interact more on the level of "who he is" and not just "what he does." Examples:

- Men's Breakfast
- Men's Retreats

- Go for the Guys Sunday

Implications: This type of gathering gives your men a taste of what can happen in a men's small group. Men's small group is an excellent next step.

Men's Small Groups

Men's small groups usually consist of 3-6 men and are designed to meet on a regular basis for discussion, prayer, and processing the Christian life. This type of entry point offers the local church increased potential for growth. Within small groups, men face the challenge of being vulnerable, helping their brothers, and encouraging men with struggles. Communication at this level moves from "what he does" and "who he is" to "what he struggles with" and "what does a man need to succeed." Examples:

- Inductive Bible Study
- Book reading and study
- Men's ministry videos

Implications: Commitment to a small group helps men resolve problems that arise from being isolated in life. They provide an environment where men can grow in Christ and where men can share ways to minister to their families, friends, church, and community.

Man-to-Man Sessions

Man-to-man sessions give a man the strongest opportunity to grow in his relationship with another man and his relationship to God. This type of ministry is built with a solid commitment to learning how to apply God's Word and relate deeper with another man. Ultimately, a man who disciples another man, one-on-one, raises up a laborer who goes into the harvest fields of men's souls. The connection between man-to-man sessions is total trust, as the mentor trains a protégé in the principles of discipleship and equipping for ministry.

Implications: Through one-on-one discipleship, men grow into mature disciples. They receive focused training and deeper accountability. Through equipping, men grow to take on more important leadership roles and responsibilities.

Guide Men through the Funnel

As a funnel provides a narrowing parameter for putting liquid into a container, so the funnel demonstrates the progression of a man's involvement in the local church. For successful progression, men must understand the need for increased commitment and biblical information. The left side of the funnel represents an increased commitment; the right side of the funnel represents increased biblical information. As the events progress down the funnel, they require a greater degree of commitment and they impart a greater degree of biblical information. The main goal of an effective ministry, to and through its men, is to help them transfer biblical truth into everyday application as they lead their families, grow in friendships, influence their churches, and change their communities. In the end, they become laborers in the harvest fields of the earth (Matthew 9:36-39).

FIGURE 2 - PROGRESSION THROUGH THE FUNNEL

Make Disciples and Disciple-Makers

All your events and efforts should have a specific purpose in building the team and ministering to your men. In Figure 3, note the upper half illustrates the strategy for making disciples. This focus is the ministry to your men. The lower half illustrates the strategy for making disciple-makers. This focus is on ministry through your men.

A man's relationship with his family reflects his true dependence on God and long-term spiritual influence. Can you imagine a church without healthy marriages (Ephesians 5:25)? Can you imagine healthy marriages without healthy men? Can you imagine healthy men without the fundamentals of the Christian faith? Having an intentional disciple-making strategy for the men of your church is the key to a truly healthy church.

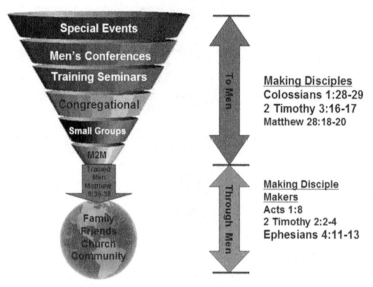

FIGURE 3 - MINISTRY TO AND THROUGH MEN

The future of your church is dependent on the next generation. Trained, godly children who are spiritually maturing will lead your church someday. "Train up a child in the way he should go, even when he is old he will not depart from it." (Proverbs 22:6) Fathers have a vital role in this process.

All that a man has is given to him by God. Men should be willing, in turn, to give to their church through their attendance, prayers, service, and financial contributions. Intentional leadership development of your men and the exercise of their spiritual gifts are essential to the health of your church (1 Peter 5:2).

The budgets, programs and the leaders of men's ministries who reflect a high commitment to outreach and evangelism, both locally and worldwide, set the pace for your church. Significant numerical growth through evangelism is an expected outcome of this commitment. As the men in your church reach out to friends, neighbors, co-workers, and others in the community, your church's ministry is multiplied (Luke 19:10).

The key principle is to make sure that all of the ongoing activities that you offer for men are helping them become disciples and disciple makers.

Define Your Ministry Purpose

Pat Morley from *Man in the Mirror* has done an outstanding job of capturing the elements that make men's ministry happen in the local church. The momentum cycle illustrates the cycles that all men's ministry goes through.

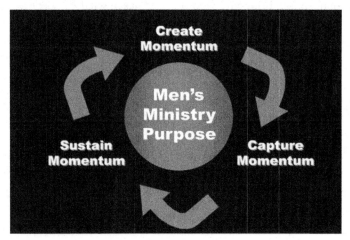

FIGURE 4 - MEN'S MINISTRY MOMENTUM CYCLE

A ministry purpose affects everything you and your ministry does. Jesus said, "Therefore go and make disciples of all nations, baptizing them in the name of the Father and the Son, and the Holy Spirit, and teaching them to obey everything I have commanded you. And surely I am with you always, to the very end of the age." (Matthew 28:19-20, NIV). The Great Commission is at the heart all the ministries in the local church. So, what is the overriding purpose of your ministry to men? It should be to make disciples who will make disciples.

The purpose of men's ministry is much greater than just helping men be better husbands, fathers, and workers. While each of these is a critical need in a man's life, they are not the biggest need nor the central reason a local church should have an effective and efficient ministry to and through its men.

A men's ministry purpose statement gives your men a clear vision and mission to all your events. The vision is the biblical mandate for ministry. It is the overarching reason you do ministry. The mission statement should bring into view the specifics of what you believe God has called you to accomplish.

The key to getting a stationary man moving is to create value for him. Know your men and their needs, and then reach them in ways that are relevant to their lives. Keep in mind that provision follows vision. Men will give to and actively support a biblical vision and mission.

Create Momentum. When you create value with an activity, you create momentum. Like a gear that makes a wheel turn so does momentum to your ministry. Typically, the first two layers of the funnel tell men what to do in their Christian lives as they help create momentum. After attending an event where they hear and learn the things to do they are ready to understand the how to do.

Capture Momentum. Capture momentum by providing the right next step. Don't create momentum without a plan for how you will capture it. Make the follow-up fit the event; choose the right size of commitment you are asking for, have an ending point, and help men take the next step. NOTE: if you consistently fail to capture momentum when you create it, you will not build a sustainable ministry. Always show men a next right step. The third and fourth layers of the funnel help men understand the how's in the Christian life. These ministries are a great way to help capture momentum.

Sustain Momentum. Sustain momentum through relationships. Men tend to fail when isolated. Together, they can become genuine disciples who can transform the world around them. First, help them uphold their spiritual progress. Second, help them with regular prayer and Bible study. The key is helping them become and stay mature in Christ.[2] The fifth and sixth layers of the funnel model provide men who will help others in their Christian lives. These layers are great ways to help continue the momentum.

FIGURE 5 - MOMENTUM APPLIED TO THE FUNNEL

Through creating, capturing, and sustaining momentum, you will increase your baseline of established disciples. However, over time you may see some men drop off. It is normal for life and ministry to happen in cycles. Some men will need several cycles to continue their growth. Not all of them will be involved in small groups or man-to-man types of events.

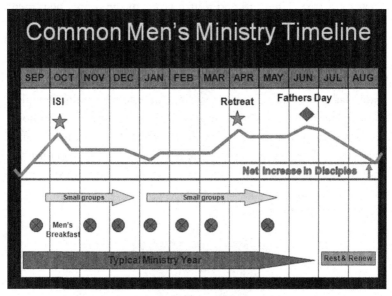

FIGURE 6 – MEN'S MINISTRY CYCLES FOR INCREASING
DISCIPLES AND DISCIPLE MAKERS

If you continue to apply these principles over time, you will have new men staying involved in your discipleship process as well as disciple makers. This includes a growing and loyal men's ministry leadership team. Each year you will have a net increase in men disciples.

Take a Survey and Identify Your Needs

Taking a survey may seem clear to some leaders; however, many leaders do not take a climate survey of the men. Surveys provide pastors and men's ministry with demographics and data that help determine which areas to focus or more important they give you the true pulse of your men and help you to see their strengths and weaknesses. Confidential surveys work and work well when applied to your battle plans for the future.

Without taking an anonymous survey of all your men, you put yourself in a position of having to guess what the men want and need. Furthermore, many men will not share openly or clearly what their needs are. Leaders often miss the mark of clearly identifying men's needs and therefore launch a ministry based on false assumptions. This has been the cause of many men's ministry failures.

Several survey options are available to a Kingdom Warrior and Iron Sharpens Iron church client. Some pastors and leaders prefer to use on-line versions while others prefer a paper-based system. This section gives you helpful tools for both options.

Online Survey Tool. Online versions provide users with quick and easy access to the survey questions as well as ensure all the questions are answered before the survey is considered complete. Users can access the system from any computer with internet access and web browser. The system is convenient and private. The weakness of this system is getting men to trust it is private and to take the time to sit at a computer and fill out the survey.

Kingdom Warrior recommends using a free or pay-to-purchase system offered by Survey Monkey.com. Survey Monkey offers a free subscription for surveys up to ten questions and one-hundred responses. Purchase plans range from $25.00 to $85.00.

Paper-Based Survey Tool. The paper based survey tool provides users with a survey that is easy to customize. Kingdom Warrior recommends using a survey that collects data using six key areas: demographics, personal development, identity with Christ, issues facing men, ministry activities and men's conferences. There are thirty questions broken into six distinct areas, plus a place for additional comments. This survey contains thirty line items, each one in soft copy that can be altered to suit your needs. Print the survey out one side only. If you do two-sided, there is a good possibility your men will not fill the back sides.

Pros for this tool include customization for local church needs, quick single point distribution, and short turn around collection. Cons are the length and need for privacy while filling them out. Some men sitting next to a spouse or other men may not feel the freedom to be candid with all of their answers. You may want to give small sections at different periods of time.

After your men complete this survey, you will have a better understanding of their:

- Demographics
- Personal development
- Identity with Christ
- Issues facing men
- Ministry activities
- Men's conferences
- Additional comments

In addition to the soft copy of the survey, is a spreadsheet for you to calculate the results. Use this as a basis for planning and justifying your plan for ministry.

Your survey should be distributed to as many of your men as possible. Some leaders opt to use mass distribution on Sunday morning and then have men drop the completed survey into a box.

As the internet and handheld technology continues to grow, so will the need for churches and ministries to leverage new tools. Be sure to check our website for the latest developments regarding surveys, automatic texts, mpegs, and downloads for ministry.

In the Surveys and Score Sheets section of this book are two surveys, one for leaders and one for all the men. The leader survey evaluates the functions of an existing team while the general survey evaluates the needs of men. After the general survey, a corresponding score sheet is provided. Both documents can be easily modified to fit the needs of a local church.

Determine Your Benchmarks and Battle Plans

Most solid disciple-making ministries, to and through men, are built over a three to five-year period. Take for example the life of Jesus. Even He took three years to start and complete His ministry. You need to take a long-range view when starting and running a quality men's ministry that is effective and efficient especially as it relates to helping men live as intentional followers of Christ. Below is a recommended four-year vision for a start-up local church men's ministry. It is only a recommendation. Each church has its own unique culture and most important its own unique men. Use this tool as a guideline for your plans.

1st Year: Get to know the men in your church. Look for men who have a heart for men's ministry. Assemble your leadership team and spend the year living for one another as an example of how you want the men in your church to live. Establish the model within your leadership team. During this year, do all your preparation work. Developing your prayer team, survey the men of your church, write a purpose statement that includes your vision and mission and get your pastor's input and support.

2nd Year: Begin to develop an identity within the church. Branding is an excellent way to market your men's ministry. You want the men who attend your church to know a ministry to men exists. Consider a logo as part of your branding. You may want to add to your leadership team and kick off one or two areas of ministry: monthly men's breakfast and an annual conference.

3rd Year: Start to expand the ministry. Be sure to include small groups if you have not done so in year 2. Pick one new area of ministry and start to plan on how you will implement it. Make it a goal for you and the leadership to identify a new ministry each year. Before beginning a new ministry offering, have a leader who is willing to be the point man. This leader should have the experience and skills necessary to develop a team of people to work with him, know the ministry purpose and have a strategy in place to implement the new ministry. During this year, your executive leadership team continues to provide training for existing leaders and new leaders for the ministry. All your men's events and ministries should support your purpose statement. If you do not sense God leading you to add to your existing ministry, that is okay, but be sure to evaluate and identify areas for improving your existing battle plan.

4th Year and Continuing: Continue to move forward and fill in any empty spots. Consider planning a leadership summit once each ministry year. This will work best if it is at the end of your ministry year, but in time to plan for next year. Evaluate each aspect of your current ministry. Identify where it is unbalanced or needs improvements. Make plans to balance the load or improve the standards. Evaluate if your leadership team is functioning properly or if it needs to be realigned with how the ministry has grown. Expect that some men on the leadership team will eventually move or switch ministries within the church. Plan for attrition by ensuring each leader works on mentoring someone else on the team. When you meet with them individually, ask them who is being prepared to take his position if he moves on. Paul had his Timothy. Timothy taught faithful men who were told to teach others (2 Timothy 2:2). By training replacements, you are preparing new leaders.

Establish Your Ministry Milestones

Here is a basic guide to help you put a strategy into place using the information you recorded in the evaluation sections. Your plan may have more or fewer goals than these samples. Keep in mind, it is better to do a few things well, than to get too spread out and do many things poorly. Consider bolting new things on each year. Locate a yearly calendar for establishing deadline dates.

Measurable Goals for Your Battle Plan – Year 1	Deadline	Deadline
1. Survey the men to determine their interests and needs		1 m
2. Identify your men's ministry leadership team		2 m

3. Develop your mission, vision, and set of guiding principles	3 m
4. Develop a prayer ministry	3 m
5. Create communication tools: cards, emails, website, newsletter…	6 m
6. Select an overall theme for your next ministry year	8 m
7. Develop a pastoral prayer ministry	8 m
8. Hold an in-house, first-class entry point type of event	10-12m

TABLE 1 – YEAR 1 SUGGESTED MILESTONES

Measurable Goals for Your Battle Plan – Year 2	Deadline
1. Establish your name and ministry logo	
2. Offer first special entry point for men on the periphery	
4. Offer second special entry point for men who frequently attend the church	
5. Develop the first phase of weekly small groups for men	
6. Identify your men's small group leaders	
7. Train your small group leaders in the dynamics for building men only groups	

TABLE 2 – YEAR 2 SUGGESTED MILESTONES

At the end of each ministry year, gather your men's ministry leadership team for a time of evaluations, prayer, preparation, and planning for the next ministry year. For many churches, most ministry activity takes place from September through June. Summers are a great time for men to get some rest, renew their spirit, and spend increased time with family.

Develop Your Battle Plan

Begin to schedule out your ministry events and assigned resources. The first quarter of a one-year battle plan for September 2016 through December 2016 from Joshua's Men, a local church, is on the following page.

MEN MINISTRY EVENT CALENDAR FOR 2016 / 2017									
Date						Title/Description	Point Man	Speaker	MPG Grub Group
Mon	Tue	Thu	Fri	Sat	Sun				
				17-Sep		Men's Breakfast	Eric Brad		NA
					25-Sep	Go for Guys Sunday - Title & Theme TBD	Brad		
		6-Oct				MPG	Mike		Jim S. Brad S.
10-Oct						Columbus Day	Holiday	NA	NA
		13-Oct				MPG	Mike		Scott D. Jim M.
				15-Oct		Men's Breakfast	Eric Brad		NA
		20-Oct				MPG	Mike		Mike R.
		27-Oct				MPG	Mike		Dennis Y.
31-Oct						Arktoberfest	ALL	NA	NA
		3-Nov				MPG	Mike		Jim S. Brad S.
				5-Nov		Iron Sharpens Iron	Brad	NA	NA
		10-Nov				MPG	Mike		Scott D. Jim M.
		17-Nov				MPG	Mike		Mike R.
				19-Nov		Men's Breakfast	Eric Brad		NA
		24-Nov				Thanksgiving		NA	NA
		1-Dec				MPG	Mike		Dennis Y.
		8-Dec				MPG	Mike		Jim S. Brad S.
		15-Dec				MPG	Mike		Scott D. Jim M.
					25-Dec	Christmas Day	ALL	NA	NA
					1-Jan	New Years Day	ALL	NA	NA
		MPG							
		Men's Breakfast							
		Holidays							
		Special Events							
		Iron Sharpens Iron							

TABLE 3 - SAMPLE MINISTRY BATTLE PLAN

It may be helpful, while completing a hard copy, to use different colored pens or markers to distinguish between the different activities. When using the soft copy, this won't be an issue. Some considerations before you plan out the entire year:

- Have a copy of the church calendar (or know the critical dates for other events).
- Have a copy of the school calendar.
- Know when each holiday is scheduled. Some holidays do not happen on the same day or week in the year.
- If possible, schedule a ministry leaders planning meeting with other leaders in your church to identify any potential schedule conflicts.
- Keep flexibility in mind. Remember "Semper Gumby" (ever flexible).

By completing the one-year calendar, your leadership team and the men of your church can see the main thrust of your men's ministry for the entire year.

Evaluate Your Effectiveness

Far too often, leaders get so busy they neglect to evaluate their effectiveness and efficiency in leading the effort to make disciples and continue with a spirit of excellence. In 1992, *Readers Digest* published an article on Joe Theismann:

Joe Theismann enjoyed an illustrious 12-year career as quarterback of the Washington Redskins. He led the team to two Super Bowl appearances—winning in 1983 before losing 0-3 the following year. When a leg injury forced him out of football in 1985, he was entrenched in the record books as Washington's all-time leading passer.

Still, the tail end of Theismann's career taught him a bitter lesson: I got stagnant. I thought the team revolved around me. I should have known it was time to go when I didn't care whether a pass hit Art Monk in the 8 or the 1 on his uniform. When we went back to the Super Bowl, my approach had changed. I was griping about the weather, my shoes, practice times, everything. Today I wear my two rings—the winner's ring from Super Bowl XVII and the loser's ring from Super Bowl XVIII. The difference in those two rings lies in applying oneself and not accepting anything but the best.[3]

Doing a great job in leading a disciple-making men's ministry requires a heart for God and a desire to seek God's best for the local church and the men. Evaluations help keep leaders from becoming narcissistic and maintain their focus on the best God has for them and for the local church.

Conduct Event Debriefs

As a general rule, a men's ministry leader should debrief the team after unique and routine events providing feedback to the group as well as to individual team members. Identify areas for improvement during the briefs and catalog them in a notebook. Key personnel should review the notes prior to the next mission and make all necessary changes for improvement. When circumstances have team members all in one location, use face-to-face communications. When this is not possible, use the best acceptable technology.

Keep Cadence with Change

As men's ministry moves into the 21st century, it will require men with vision and know-how who can make the necessary shifts and adapt to rapid changes in the way men communicate. Already, men with sons in high-school or college are learning to text message as a routine form of communication.

Along with rapid changes in technology, creative leaders will need to find creative ways for men to relate with one another. The function of the church has not changed since Christ uttered His famous words in Matthew 28:18-20.

Technology to consider with men:

- Routine emails
- Blogs
- Tweets
- Tablets, smartphones, and PDA's

In Summary

Providing quality training for men in a disciple-making ministry helps them develop their skills and knowledge base, as well as equipping them to do the job properly. Never ask a man to do anything you aren't willing to train him to do, or for that matter, do yourself.

One-on-one. One-on-one training allows for the greatest level of impact and change in a man's life. Through one-on-one, a mentor and protégé exchange dialogue, explore situations and answer personal questions, all of which may not happen in a small group setting. The following four principles of one-on-one give the mentor a clear method for imparting both knowledge and skills in another man to equip him for ministry.

- Tell him why: Explain why this task is important to the man, to the team and to the Lord.

- Show him how: Before giving him the task, have the man watch you complete the task as it is properly accomplished.
- Get him started: Whenever possible, work with and alongside a man before asking him to do a job by himself.
- Keep him going: After the man takes on the new role and responsibilities, be sure to periodically discuss the assignment and view the results.

Small groups. Small groups are extremely effective in training more than one man. As men grow in their relationships, they become more like Christ. Leadership is developed as men move from acquaintances to friends to brothers. A by-product of helping men develop leadership in a small-group setting is giving preliminary experience to each man that leads. This is very beneficial in the future when they are called to lead a small group of their own.

Books. There are several excellent books on starting, building, and growing men's ministry. Reading a book and meeting to discuss the content is a great way to provide all the leaders with a common foundation of service and ministry. In some individual situations, giving a book helps one or two of your men gain insight into specific men's ministry related issues. You can find a list of recommended books at www.kingdomwarrior.net

Magazines, periodicals, emails. Besides books, you can use magazines, periodicals, and online emails to disseminate information to the leadership team. Ask your pastor to pass on any good articles to you for review and forwarding to the team.

Videos and DVDs. DVDs and videos are excellent tools that give men a medium that appeals to a man's visual senses. In addition, the majority of DVD series do not require extensive preparations. Leaders can review the materials, insert the DVD, and join the team to view the contents.

Seminars/conferences. Many regional and denominational conferences provide excellent messages, seminars, and workshops that focus on specific issues related to life and ministry.

Delegate, don't abdicate. Delegation is the assignment of authority and responsibility to another person to carry out specific activities. However, the person who delegated the work remains accountable for the outcome of the assigned work. It allows a protégé to make decisions independently—a shift of decision-making authority from the mentor to the mentee. The opposite of effective delegation is micromanagement, where a manager provides too much input, direction, and review of the delegated work. Your ministry will only develop and grow as you invest in leaders and delegate the ministry roles and responsibilities.

Transfer and release. Men need authority, freedom, and resources to perform as God has gifted them. To develop leaders, start small and build up with increasing responsibility and authority. Give them a small task to accomplish before assigning a large one. Evaluate their performance, make appropriate suggestions, and learn from their effort—how they work, operate and relate to others. Teach them to analyze and solve their problems.

- What has to be done?
- When will it be done?
- Who will help?
- What tools or resources will the task require?

Give them your time, talents, and treasures

- Be willing to expand your resources for them
- Be a servant to them whenever possible
- Be available to assist them as required
- Ask them questions about their ministry: "How it is going? "What do you need?" "Is there anything you would like assistance with?" Help them identify bottlenecks or potential problems before completing a task. Provide necessary feedback.

Stay in touch. Establish communication plans with your leaders. You need to be routinely available to meet with your men to discuss how they are doing both in their personal and ministerial lives. As you give away aspects of your ministry, be available to support and encourage their hard work as men labor in the harvest fields. Find out how you can serve them and make them successful.

Celebrate victories and change. At least once a year, take the time to review the ministry to identify the successes over your ministry year. Calculate the lives that were touched and men that were changed as a result of the men's ministry. Set up up a celebration dinner or BBQ. Pass out awards and gifts with a significant emphasis on thanking them for building up God's kingdom.

CHAPTER

3

Building a Men's Ministry Team

By Tom Cheshire

There is nothing new under the sun, Solomon declared in Ecclesiastes 1:9. "What has been is what will be, and what has been done is what will be done, and there is nothing new under the sun." This chapter illustrates that truth. The concept that effective leadership is never done alone is not new. Jethro spoke it to his son-in-law Moses, but even more effective is the model that we see Jesus implement as He begins His ministry. He calls twelve men to join him. Neither of these examples negates the fact that one man is the leader, but it does show the principle that they both saw and understood — they needed other men around them to move the mission forward.

I hope everything covered in this chapter will encourage you as you seek to develop a disciple-making ministry to the men in your church. Much of what you will read here is a skeleton to which you and your team will put meat on. The reality is that every church has DNA. It has a heritage; it has a lineage that will make the end ministry look a little different, just like each of us as children of God look a little different.

This truth only reinforces the necessity of a team for the overall success of this ministry.

This book and this chapter will not solve or answer every question you might have about ministry to men. Ministry to men is hard work, if it weren't, then more would be doing it, and so many would not have tried and given up. G.K. Chesterton said, "If it is worth doing, it is worth doing badly." This line is not an excuse for poor efforts. It is perhaps an excuse for poor results. Our society is plagued by wanting good results with no efforts (or rather, with someone else's efforts). We hire someone else to work for us, to play for us (that is, to entertain us), to think for us, and to raise our children for us. We have left "the things worth doing" to others on the poor excuse that others might be able to do them better. This sums up individual discipleship and ripples out to bring us to where we are today in developing a disciple-making ministry to and for our men.

My desire in this chapter is to both make the biblical case for why a leadership team is non-negotiable, as well as demonstrate what the function and structure of the team might look like. This comes from my personal journey as a man and as a leader in my own church as well as hundreds of hours of conversations with pastors, men's leaders and men who want to reach and equip their men. I have tried to be a one-man show and even had limited success at that, but ultimately it is not sustainable. The mission of Matthew 28:18-20 where Jesus came and said to them, "All authority in heaven and on earth has been given to me. Go therefore and make disciples of all nations, baptizing them in the name of the Father, the Son, and the Holy Spirit, teaching them to observe all that I have commanded you. And behold, I am with you always, to the end of the age," is too great for one man. Moses and a host of other lesser men like me have tried, and it never ended well.

If you are reading this chapter, I could make a couple assumptions. One assumption is that you know the team model is the correct way to build a sustainable disciple-making ministry, and you are looking for key elements of this model. The other assumption is that you really believe you can do this alone. Either way, I pray this book will help you yield to the Holy Spirit to see the value in the model Jesus gave us and seek to bring men around you who also desire to see men impacted through your local church's ministry to men. The underlying hope in this chapter is that you will see the value and biblical model of the leadership team. That will successfully lead to the development of others to not only lead but to replace us as leaders so we can serve and glorify God in other areas in the local church.

We all have a limit to the time we are here, and only God knows when that time is up. Having the right team model helps us to not only grow personally but to pass the torch of leadership that will outlast us. Teams are more likely to build legacies than individuals. We see this in what Jesus started during His earthly ministry and then passed on to the 11 original disciples that spread the gospel around the world. The Apostle Paul summed this mission up in 2 Timothy 2:2, "...and what you have heard from me in the presence of many witnesses entrust to faithful men who will be able to teach others also."

Please don't look at building a team as an end to achieve a sustainable disciple-making ministry to men; rather, look at it as investing the gospel in other men that will then invest the gospel in other men. As wide as our personal wisdom may be, it is impossible to think we alone could effectively reach all the men in our church, let alone those men outside our churches. However, a team of men, each with his own gifts and abilities (diversities), can more effectively reach men we never could. The ultimate purpose for man is to glorify God, so how much more might we glorify God as a team than if we were alone.

Jesus was the Son of the living God and He understood this when He said, "Truly, truly, I say to you, whoever believes in me will also do the works that I do; and greater works than these will he do because I am going to the Father." (John 14:12). My heart and goal, as a resource to the local church, is that this ministry to men would create and develop a culture that makes disciples, that make disciples.

The Critical Team Members

1. The pastor
2. The men's leader
3. The diverse team members

Before we get too far, I want to state the obvious because we don't want to take some of the basics and obvious things for granted. A church's mission to make disciples is God's vision for the church. I know I have been guilty of trying to fit everything under ministry to men because that is how God reached me and it put me on the course to be a resource for men in the local church.

I am not saying women and children are not important and there isn't any value in seeing women and children come to know Christ and grow in their knowledge and understanding of God, His word and application in their lives. I can assure you, having a wife for 33 years and two daughters, I see women as equal heirs of equal value in the Kingdom. However, I do see from the beginning of God's word, men and women were given roles and responsibilities before the fall and it is not my desire to have someone read this and think otherwise.

The other obvious point I want to make is that this all must be bathed in prayer and yielded to the power that is in us as believers. We cannot accomplish anything of value outside of God's will and the Holy

Spirit's power, nothing that will ultimately glorify God. John makes that very clear in John 15:5, "I am the vine; you are the branches. Whoever abides in me and I in him, he it is that bears much fruit, for apart from me you can do nothing." Jesus goes on to give us a great promise and the results are just a few verses later in John 15:7-8 with these words, "If you abide in me, and my words abide in you, ask whatever you wish, and it will be done for you. By this, my Father is glorified, that you bear much fruit and so prove to be my disciples."

With that said, we must always remember, apart from prayer, Christ, and the Holy Spirit we can do nothing. We can't do this on our own strength and I believe that is part of the reason developing a sustainable ministry to men has not been as effective as it could be. So heed this caution, regardless of which team member you are, if you are not fully submitting to Christ and the power of the Holy Spirit, stop right now and make that relationship right. Rick Warren said it well in The Purpose Driven Life, "It's not about you."

OK, there may be more "obvious" statements we need to make going forward, but for now, let's get started with who makes up this team.

The Pastor

The pastor: who exactly is that? This may be argued and debated, but my experience and seeing variations of who this is has shown that the pastor has the greatest impact, over any other man in the church, on the success and sustainability of men's ministry. I know we have tried to lower the bar in this area when meeting with churches and it has always ended with failure. Without the pastor being an active part of this team, you can have the most on fire men's leader and an incredibly diverse team and it will eventually run its course and fade away. If the pastor does not believe growing his men is paramount to building

Christ's church, it is a lock that at some point it will fail. I wish it weren't true, but it has been proved too many times over the years. While there are other contributors to this roller coaster effect, the lack of the pastor's active engagement is the most significant.

Yes, we are aware of books and curriculums that parse the importance of this role, and we have personally bought into this in the past trying to make it work without him. The reality has been overwhelming; we cannot move off this one. Without this being bathed in prayer and yielding to the Holy Spirit, we are doing it on our own strength and Jesus was very clear where that would land us. I will relent somewhat on how much the pastor needs to be involved, but I won't relent that he must be fully committed to seeing men discipled and grown in Christ. The truth is that the pastor must be actively investing in men outside of his role in this team.

The bottom line is the pastor is not the leader of your ministry to men. He is, however, the catalyst of it. The men's leader and the team need to know the pastor is committed both personally and corporately to discipleship. They also need to know that he is committed to the long haul and not going to pull the plug on it. They need to know he is going to support it with ministry funding along with his personal involvement. I don't think he has to be at every leadership team meeting or function the ministry does, but in the early stages is the best time for him to build relationships and confidence in the leadership. This, however, is a negotiable length of time that the pastor and men's leader can and should agree on. This level of detail is, in some part, what I referred to earlier as putting meat on the bones of the skeleton. The nature of this chapter again is not to go into detail of the roles of each of the team, rather, to put together the framework/skeleton of the team.

Summary of the pastor as a team member:

1. Must be actively discipling men
2. Must be an active participant in the development and sustainability of the ministry to men
3. Must be committed to the long haul
4. Must help secure financial support of the church for the ministry

The Men's Leader

Next to the pastor, this is a key role to the success, sustainability and development of a healthy ministry to men. It may be that this person is part of the paid staff, but most likely, this man is a lay leader. If your church is large enough that it has a staff person specifically for the men, great, but in most of the churches I work with, this position is a layman. One of the key attributes of this man is that he is a leader, not that he can't be early on or "young" in leadership, but does he have the marks of a leader.

It is worth mentioning that not every man that says, "I want to lead something," is in fact gifted as a leader. If you are reading this and you think you are the man for this men's leader role, I would encourage you to have some assessments done that put you in the leadership group, as well as having others affirm this trait in you. If you are a pastor reading this, then I would ask that you vet him for leadership gifts and not just settle for the one man who raises his hand or throws his name in the hat. Remember, one of the sub-cultures I desire in all of this is to help men see their roles as replaceable or replicated so as they serve, they are grooming others to step up or into a deeper leadership role. This is the implication of 2 Timothy 2:2: I have determined you are a faithful man, so I invest (disciple) you, you will then go on to discern other faithful men and invest them. I can also take this back to Jesus' model. He selected the 12, invested in them and then gave them (and us) the great commission to go and invest in others.

The older I become and the more I work with churches, the more I see Jesus' model as the perfect model. While there are many different aspects of ministry to men in the church, this is the basis of all we do: moving men into these roles and growing men (sanctification) in Christ. I will flush some of this out later on in this chapter as well as other chapters in this book.

This may fall into the stating the obvious category, but this man needs to be on fire for Christ and right behind that passion, he needs to be passionate for men. I remember being introduced as "Tom is a man who has a passion for men!" Once the introduction stopped, I said I just needed to clarify that I have a passion for men, to see them grown in Christ. Seriously, this should be a man who wakes up each day desiring to help men know Christ, grow in Christ and see men's lives transformed by the gospel. This is critical. The reality is that this work is hard and if Christ has not called you to this with a God-sized passion for other men, you will quit before you reach the finish line.

The men's leader needs to have a strong vision. He needs to be able to understand the primary vision of the pastor and his church and then help dream and cast the vision of how the disciple-making ministry to the men not only fits into the churches vision but also compliments it. This man needs to be someone who understands the pastor's vision and mission for the church, is in full agreement with it and desires nothing more than to be a part of accomplishing it personally and supporting it with the ministry to the church's men! Sad is the man who somehow thinks his vision for the ministry to men is more important than the church's vision. Unfortunately, this is a byproduct when the pastors are not part of the team.

Another good filter to use, for both the men's leader and the team members, is whether or not they are HOT. No, I'm not talking George Clooney or Ryan Gosling! HOT is an acronym for honest, open and transparent. We aren't looking for the perfect man, but as we examine those men and assemble this group, we do need to have some criteria. We select men who have enough spiritual maturity that they understand this is not about them, but about glorifying God. Men who are generally honest about who they are and who they aren't and are open and know that confession and repentance go a long way in working with others are the leaders we want. They understand Philippians 2:1-11. They know that they don't have all the answers and they defer to others who may have the answer or a better solution. They know when they misstep; they can admit it. The apostle Paul gives us examples in his life as recorded in the New Testament. We see this in Romans 7:15-20 where Paul clearly models his struggle in sanctification by confessing that he too struggles with the flesh. In 1 Timothy 1:15, Paul again confesses his past and what he used to be (Acts 9). Perhaps one of the best examples is in 2 Timothy 4:11 where Paul asks for John Mark, who he had clearly dismissed back in Acts 13:13, Paul shows his maturity in his willingness to reconcile a past wrong.

This next one will apply to both the leader and the team members and might be easily misunderstood, but I hope to clarify it. They need to be more of an 'equipper' than a 'doer.' I know when I make that statement, some men wrestle with it because they think I am saying they are excluded from work. That is not what I'm saying. It isn't that cooking or setting up chairs, emptying the trash, and a host of other chores are somehow below the leader and leadership team. What I am saying is that because of the heavy lifting of the planning and execution of these tasks, they can't be fully 'equipper' and 'doer'. Men who are investing the time to be the strategic planners of developing and fitting all the various pieces of this ministry together can't be the primary workers too. Another point to help explain what I am talking about is that the whole of the team, as part of the disciple-making culture, sees these entry points, such as cooking, setting-up, etc., as roles to engage men in their gifts and abilities.

Summary of the men's leader as a team member:

1. Must be actively discipling men
2. Must be a man who is gifted in leadership
3. Needs to have a deep passion for reaching and equipping men
4. Needs to be strong vision caster

The Diverse Team

I have purposefully been referring to the leadership team as the diverse team because that is what we know to be the most effective way to understand this group of men. The size of this group will vary from church to church, so we set no right or wrong or even a suggested number for that reason. Logically, you understand that the more men you have in your church, the more men might populate this team. However, just because you have hundreds of men in your church, doesn't mean your team should be large. Perhaps the other caution is, just because your church is small doesn't mean you don't need a team. Regardless of the size of your church, this decision, like all decisions, need to be committed to prayer, seeking the discernment of the Holy Spirit as you seek to engage the men who you see God raising up to serve Christ in this ministry. Remember, we can't do this on our own strength; this has to be something we do from obedience to God's will in our life. This is also another reason why the pastor's active involvement in this ministry is critical. The men's leader and pastor should be on their knees working together very closely with whom they see God bringing up to help them grow in faith and leadership.

Many of the traits I shared in the men's leader section apply to the men who would be on this diverse team, so I won't go back over them. Just go back up and read them and apply them as they fit the men on the diverse leadership team.

Our encouragement here, even though it is pretty obvious in the definition, is that this group needs to be diverse. Diverse is, as diverse does! While multi-cultural, multi-ethnical churches do exist, but we wish more did. You obviously would apply cultural and ethnical diversity if you are in one of these churches, but for most, diversity is going to equate out to age and gifting. The rule here is: your diverse team should look like the church and those you desire to reach. If your team is all 50 and above and you desire to reach the younger men, you are most likely not going to be effective doing so. As a white, 60-year-old man, I desire to reach younger men. My ideas and plans will most likely not land as well as they would if I had a 20 or 30 something-year-old man to give a voice to on the leadership team and sought his ideas on how and what we might do to engage younger men effectively.

This point is played out in every way you may have diversity in the men in your church. If you have a diverse church and you want to grow the church more in those areas, then look for a man to join the team who is part of that ethnic or cultural area. If you have a desire to reach more Hispanic men, then you will be more likely to succeed if you have a Hispanic man or men on the team. I don't want to limit the power of God and say if you are a team of white dudes, you could never reach men of any other ethnicity, but someone on the team will have to intentionally and purposely pursue that relationship outside the team to garner the insight of how the church can be more effective.

Sadly, in the course of the years I have been doing this, I have met a lot of grumpy old men who don't want to reach out to younger men because no one gave them a chance, or walked alongside them to help them navigate life and what it meant to be a godly man. "Nobody helped me, so let them figure it out on their own!" Unfortunately, those men are a part of churches that are dying and closing their doors in large part to their hard hearts.

Regardless of hard hearts like this or a host of other ways we have closed our hearts off to God, we pray that there will be men on your team who see the great value not only in investing in men but in men that are different than them. Men on this team have to realize that as good as your way was and as effective as it was 10, 20, or 30 years ago, we need to be open to new ideas, willing to listen to men younger than us and heaven forbid even allow them to fail. We need to have a safe environment that allows for failure. When we do, and failures occur, we use it to humble ourselves, see what God is teaching us, and grow stronger, rather than bitter or passive.

A healthy and diverse team will accomplish more for the glory of God than any of us could ever accomplish alone.

Summary of the men who will make up the diverse team:

1. Must be actively discipling men
2. Have leadership qualities
3. Strategic thinkers
4. Represent the diverse cross-section of men in your church

Function of the Team

I gave some of the skeleton and maybe even a little meat in the previous section of the chapter on the function of the team and its individual members. I will flush out the function using the three categories below to help strengthen the framework or skeleton.

1. Vision
2. Strategy
3. Implementation

These three are not exclusive and there will be nuances that I will cover here too, but remember that with each church the DNA will be a factor in this area as well. It has been my experience that when we agree and develop these functions well, most, if not all the other functions fit.

Vision

The vision of this ministry must fit and further the larger vision of the church. The vision does need to be big and requires God be in it to achieve it. I help churches define vision as, "where do you want to be…God-sized" and mission answers the question of what do we do now and going forward to get there? The team that works together to listen to God and looks at the men in their church to form this vision is a team that will then "see" how they accomplish it. I have not used a vision statement until now because the vision statement comes after you have reached a consensus on what the vision is. The vision statement then becomes a working phrase that helps cast the vision to all the other men. Patrick Morley in his books *The Man in the Mirror* and *No Man Left Behind* helped me understand the importance of communicating that this ministry to men is for all the men in your church. They use the terms inclusive verses, exclusive language, which has made a huge impact on how I speak and come alongside churches. Please don't overlook the magnitude of this paradigm shift.

For some reading this book, you may have an existing men's ministry and be skimming through this book to see if you can pick up any nuggets that may help you. This would be one of those nuggets. Pull your team together and honestly ask, "Do we communicate our vision that this ministry is to and for all the men in our church? Do the things we do combine to help men see value for them because of what our ministry offers and calls them to?" Here is my example of how the light bulb went off in my head from this paradigm.

Years ago, I was the men's ministry leader in my church and our main function for the men was a monthly breakfast. I used to invite all the men, but many men never came. I was personally offended and held bitterness toward men who I knew well in my church but never came. After all, this was our men's ministry and they were men, so why did they not see that and come? What I was missing was that many of the men whom I was angry at were serving as deacons, trustees, worship leaders, Sunday school teachers, etc. My problem was I looked at men's ministry as an exclusive event, group, or function. This exclusive paradigm in my mind negated the fact that these men were serving in other key roles in the church because they weren't attending my breakfast. Even though they were men, I didn't feel like they were part of the men's ministry in our church.

The inclusive paradigm is that wherever men are serving, there is men's ministry. The vision of the ministry to men is such that all men see themselves as part of the ministry, regardless if they ever come to a monthly breakfast or any other function. Hopefully, light bulbs are going off all over the place as you read this! The reality is, as I travel around and meet with churches, the exclusive mindset still seems to be the predominant paradigm in most churches.

This exclusive paradigm knows no denominational or non-denominational barriers! My own denomination, SBC, is a prime example of pigeon holing men's ministry in exclusive categories like Disaster Relief. You need to hear my heart here; I am not saying the monthly breakfast or incredible ministries like Disaster Relief are not valuable and worthy for men to be a part of and lead well in. But, they are not in and of themselves ministry to or for all the men who serve in other ways. I have used the term entry points previously in this chapter and I would say these and other exclusive ministry opportunities are entry points to connect and engage men. Hopefully, not only are light bulbs going off as you see the paradigm shift from exclusive to inclusive, but also that you understand the huge importance that vision plays in communicating to your team that all men are important.

Strategy

The leadership team (all 3 elements) has the formidable task of developing a strategy that helps build a culture of discipleship throughout a ministry driven by the mission that is achieved by what you are doing now and in going forward. Whether you are starting from scratch, revamping an existing ministry that has stalled or trying to tweak an active, vibrant ministry to men, the leadership team bears the responsibility.

One of the things I tell pastors who we meet with very early on is that most men's ministries are not strategic or intentional. I try to encourage pastors and men's leaders to be honest and admit to this, not dwelling on the fact they are failing, but to encourage them to make changes going forward. Why is this so hard? In any existing church, this new effort to be strategic and intentional is like changing a tire on a moving vehicle. The reality is, all existing churches are moving vehicles and there may be wisdom in putting the men's ministry in the pits or even better, in the garage, so we can safely put it up on the lift, maintain it, and then roll it out. Communicate to all the men what is going on and build great anticipation by keeping the lines of communication open as your team is overhauling the ministry. Then make a big splash when you roll the ministry out, once the vehicle is road worthy.

The strategy the leadership team is working on includes things such as looking honestly at what you are doing now. During that review, there may be some things you need to kill. It should also include things that are working well. While strategizing, also look at things such as what entry points do we offer where men can get onto the discipleship road. What things do we offer men to get healthy? What things do we offer our men to grow stronger? What do we have to help develop leaders? What do we have for men who are leaders to help them be more effective? When the leadership team is praying and looking honestly at these, I suggest a question to use to help make hard decisions. "Are we doing things that are making disciples and have a discipleship element to them?" The summation of being strategic and intentional in light of vision and mission is to see every man in a discipleship relationship with at least one other man. The question then, is, "What are we doing to move every man in that direction?" If my vision is to run in the Boston Marathon, my strategy is that I obviously need to start running and I need to have a plan of how many days I run, how far, what I should eat, what I shouldn't eat, etc.

Implementation

The work of implementation adds to the justification of why the leadership team is the primary equippers rather than the doers.

Remember that we are not saying that anyone or everyone on the leadership team is exempt from setting up chairs, or serving in the things that we are doing, but they should not be the primary ones because their job, if you will, is developing the plan (strategy) and executing those plans (implementation). It would also be why I would make the case that part of the leadership team's responsibility is developing their replacement so they can either go on and lead in other ways or maybe take off time from leadership and rest to be better equipped themselves.

So what does implementation look like? Great question! I am not trying to be elusive, but quite honestly, it will ultimately look different in almost every church because of the whole DNA thing again. If we go back to the example of the Boston Marathon being our vision and we need to be strategic and intentional, then implementation is carrying out the running regime, and diet plan. I think there are some basics rules that will apply regardless of your DNA. One of those is keeping it simple; less is more. I tend to think the opposite; the more complex or the more I offer, the better. I use rhythm as a term for implementation, which your church may already use, call it something else or never gave it a name.

The idea here is that there is a systematic approach to all that you offer with periods of time in between where men are not being asked or offered something. There are different ideas and terminology that those like MITM, Kenny Luck and others who have books and curriculums designed to help churches establish sustainable disciple-making ministries to men use. I have tried to use ideas and terminology from those ministries as well as our own language. What we can all agree on, as far as implementation goes, is that we know our men and offer ways to reach and equip our men.

The key is working from our vision and being strategic and intentional in all we do. The amount and variety of things we offer should have a rhythm, so we offer a couple large group gatherings in a yearly cycle. We then connect those with clear pathways that move men along the spiritual growth continuum (sanctification) that helps our men become more like Christ. What those large group gatherings consist of, as well as the different forms of equipping, is up to you. I use the following example to help churches see the key of implementation of a strategy to move men along in both spiritual growth and deeper relationships with the men of their church. I use the Iron Sharpens Iron Men's Equipping Conference as the large group gathering of many of your men. This type of event is an easy entry point for the men to get on the spiritual growth continuum. It is an easy way for men to get to know one another better (relational).

As part of the strategy, the leadership team has already prepared how to move men along the spiritual growth continuum by having everything in place to offer the men a 6-week men's study immediately after they get back from the conference. This can be something like a Men's Fraternity Series 33 study. The idea here is you have captured the energy from the large group and immediately offered them something that will be a little more relational (small groups) as well as a little deeper spiritually. Then, out of the end of the 6-week study, the team already has some opportunities and challenges for the men to go deeper spiritually and relationally again! This could be something like challenging men to connect with 3-4 other men from this study or a few men in the church they know to meet weekly for an hour. The team will have one or two suggestions as to what this time might look like. It could be agreeing to read 1 John and discuss what God revealed to them about themselves, their life, etc. It could be a short book on discipleship that helps them see even better the biblical implications of discipleship. The idea is that you are moving men to deeper relational levels with other men as well as deeper spiritual levels.

Ministries like Relevant Practical Ministry for Men (RPM), Noble Warriors, Focal Point Ministries and others around the country can and do desire to help you determine which of these might be a good fit. These ministries and others have taught and facilitated many different books and curriculums and therefore can give you great coaching in men's discipleship. The good news is you aren't alone and there are others who are out there to help you be successful at both reaching and equipping you and your men.

Defensible Structure

The last section of this chapter is what I call a defensible structure. It is the culmination of what the leadership team needs once you have formed the team, developed or refined the vision of the church into a ministry vision. Then put a strategy together and have begun implementation to the men.

1. Measurables
2. Transparency
3. Accountability

Measurables

I quoted a passage from John 15:7-8 earlier, here it is again. "If you abide in me, and my words abide in you, ask whatever you wish, and it will be done for you. By this, my Father is glorified, that you bear much fruit and so prove to be my disciples." I think it is fair to say Jesus put some measurables on His disciples as well as us. I have read somewhere that if Jesus was graded on what we in America call success, numerical growth, material possessions as well as monetary significance, then He was a failure. Rather, Jesus said success would produce much fruit thereby proving to be His disciples. I am not saying if you have a large church, multiple campuses and revenues in the millions that you are not producing much fruit. However, the thought that keeps me up at night and motivates me to do what I do is, if our churches were producing fruit, i.e., disciples that prove they are His disciples, then wouldn't our communities and culture look different.

If we can't agree that the primary mission of the church is found in Matthew 28:18-20, then we probably will differ on what a successful ministry to men in our churches should look like and how we should measure how we are doing.

Others, who are much smarter and have far more wisdom than I have, believe that making disciples is the central mission of every church. As I wrap this chapter up, I hope that everything in this chapter and the rest of this book helps you not only understand this but make it a reality.

With that, how we measure success has to be tangible. Not that we live for statistics, but that we see fruit being produced. Fruit can have several facets, but as a baseline, we would put forth that it is 2 Timothy 2:2. We have men who we have discipled and life-on-life discipleship that is producing other men who then go on to disciple other men. Maybe you look at your church now and can say yes to this statement. Our church is seeing men being discipled and they are then going out and discipling other men. If so, then praise God; you have a successful disciple-making ministry to men in your church. If you are not able to say that about your church, then our prayer is that not only this chapter, but also this book will help you crack that code, be successful by God's standards, and move in that direction.

I wish that in my personal life as well as my church, this growth and fruit production would happen quicker, but the reality is this spiritual growth issue is slow and hard work. We need to be honest and have some measurables to help us persevere as we are discipled and as we disciple others.

There are some facets that we can look to that help us measure spiritual growth that occurs simultaneously as we are seeking to make disciples. We can look at some other markers such as, how are areas in our men's lives, like marriages, finances, parenting, church unity to name a few, doing. Hopefully, we could agree that if we are successful at moving men along the spiritual growth continuum, we should see it in how they are leading in their homes with their wives and children, how they are being godly employees and employers, and how they are stewarding their resources, time, money and material possessions.

I think there are numerous scriptures that might help us as we seek to determine how our men and we are growing. Obviously, Christ is always our standard, not each other. Here are some scriptures that you may find useful.

1 Corinthians 11:1, Paul says "Be imitators of me, as I am of Christ." Are the men imitating Christ and are their lives imitate-able?

Colossians 1:10-11, "...so as to walk in a manner worthy of the Lord, fully pleasing to him, bearing fruit in every good work and increasing in the knowledge of God. May you be strengthened with all power, according to his glorious might, for all endurance and patience with joy."

Philippians 1:27, "Only let your manner of life be worthy of the gospel of Christ, so that whether I come and see you or am absent, I may hear of you that you are standing firm in one spirit, with one mind striving side by side for the faith of the gospel." Are our lives worthy of the calling, worthy of the gospel?

For 1 Timothy 3:1-13, most Bibles have a heading that reads "qualifications for elders and deacons" which is true, but in reality, they are qualifications all men should aspire to. We may be tempted to use other measurables, and while some may be helpful, our fruit needs to line up with how God's word defines what a disciple of Christ looks like. It should give us comfort that success isn't having 500 men attending something, while that would be good and we can use that as an entry point, it is more about what are we doing to measure those 500 men in their spiritual growth continuum.

Transparency

A major aspect of transparency is first being honest about yourself. The reality is, the pastor, men's leader and the team members are all in the process of working out their salvation with fear and trembling.

Philippians 2:12, "Therefore, my beloved, as you have always obeyed, so now, not only as in my presence but much more in my absence, work out your own salvation with fear and trembling." If we are going to help lead our men, then we must set the model of what this looks like, first among the leadership team and then to the men.

Luke 12:4-5, "I tell you, my friends, do not fear those who kill the body, and after that have nothing more that they can do. But I will warn you whom to fear: fear him who, after he has killed, has authority to cast into hell. Yes, I tell you, fear him!" In our desire to be transparent, remember that it is not man we fear but God.

Lastly, for personal encouragement of what transparency should look like, 2 Corinthians 13:5-7 says, "Examine yourselves, to see whether you are in the faith. Test yourselves. Or do you not realize this about yourselves, that Jesus Christ is in you?—unless indeed you fail to meet the test! I hope you will find out that we have not failed the test. But we pray to God that you may not do wrong—not that we may appear to have met the test, but that you may do what is right, though we may seem to have failed."

When we use truth to help us personally remember what is important, this will communicate to those we are seeking to lead. The transparency on a ministry level is also closely related to the ability to admit mistakes and not bring condemnation from the team and the men, but build humility and trust. Where we have healthy transparency, we have a safe environment to try things and fail, which will lead to a greater advancement of the gospel and glory to God.

Jesus himself had moments of frustration with His 12 and I would say some were epic failures. Peter said he would never let Jesus die and all of them fell asleep in the garden of Gethsemane. Therefore, whether it is those on the leadership team or the men you are discipling, we can and will have failures. We are, after all, talking about men here! The ability to be ultimately transparent in everything is trusting in the promises of God's grace and knowing that in our weakness Jesus is sufficient!

Accountability

The link between transparency and accountability is huge. Neither can be as good alone as they are in concert with one another. I started this section with measurables and how it is a fruit producing inspection. So, to be real and honest, our flesh will tend to lead us into not having measurables or simply wanting to look good. The health of us as men and as leaders is found in being accountable to one another. How do we expect to hold accountable those we desire to lead, both inside the leadership team and outside to the larger group of the men in our church, if we don't have others that we are accountable to? What we create if we don't have a healthy accountability, is at best a shell of what appears to be integrity or worse, a completely false narrative that everything is well and right, when it is actually a mess.

We need to keep the vision and mission in front of us; again, I hope we agree we find our vision and mission in Mathew 28:18-20. Our vision needs to be centered in the gospel and to make disciples. Discipleship is relational, so in healthy relationships we have accountability. The ministry of discipleship to our men will then also be relational, so the ways we are accountable in this ministry will create a healthy model of accountability as well.

We are called to live lives of submission, honoring others more than ourselves. We do this by being accountable first to God.

Romans 14:12, "So then each of us will give an account of himself to God." Much like the passages we looked at for transparency, these scriptures help us see the connection that bonds these two areas is confession. We have great hope when we see by confessing to one another that God is trustworthy to forgive us and heal us!

James 5:16, "Therefore, confess your sins to one another and pray for one another, that you may be healed. The prayer of a righteous person has great power as it is working."

A Word of Encouragement

My hope is that this chapter has given you some sturdy handles to grab a hold of to help you understand how important the leadership team is in the execution of developing a sustainable disciple-making ministry to your men. My greatest hope is that I have presented this from the perspective that this, like the entire book, is for the glory of God and not ours. The need that all this be bathed in prayer from the beginning and throughout the development, implementation and execution is only by the power of the Holy Spirit, not our own strength. The pastor, the men's leader and each team member must be fully dependent on Jesus.

I desire that this chapter and book be a source of encouragement to see the need to disciple men, both personally and as a ministry. I believe that it must begin with the pastor. If you are a pastor reading this, please know we desire that you be honest and examine your heart in relation to Mathew 28:18-20. I know the immense responsibility you have to shepherd the flock God has given you. I do not discount the need for you to preach and teach each week as you bring God's word to bear on those entrusted to your care. I don't take for granted the incredible task of counseling those who you serve and ministering to the sick, and all that you are asked to do day in and day out. I do believe that to completely delegate discipleship to others is a temptation. However, at the basic level, you as a pastor are a disciple too and thereby called to disciple others.

Our senior pastor is Jesus Christ, He is our perfect model, and He first chose 12 men who He would disciple for the 3 years of His ministry. Yes, He preached and taught to the masses, healed the sick, but He knew the value and necessity to disciple. May we encourage you to do the same. If you are doing this, then you know the fruit it is bearing and how it is making you a better pastor and growing you too. When we look at John 17:4, we see Jesus praying to the Father, "I glorified you on earth, having accomplished the work that you gave me to do." We see Him expressing to the Father that His work is complete. While that is clearly pointing to the finished work He was about to complete on the cross, it should also be some encouragement that He then goes directly into praying for His disciples and for their work of carrying on the mission.

This chapter is based on the very truth that we are called to glorify God, which is man's purpose. While there are many aspects to how we glorify God, we believe that by making disciples that make disciples, is at the center of everything else we do in our service to God. We have tried to give some practical ways this is played out in the church and investing in men is paramount. I stated in the beginning that we couldn't do this on our own strength. We need God to accomplish this. We trust God will use this chapter and this book to cast not only a vision for this, but give you scripture and real ways you can accomplish this in your church.

If you are a men's leader or someone who desires to see a disciple-making ministry in your church, I hope that this will encourage you to pray for your pastor, come alongside him and support his vision for your church. If your church has a culture of making disciples that make disciples, I pray this chapter and book will be a resource to how you build a strong team that helps the pastor achieve the great commission. This is not about us men and not so others will see how great we are, but that the world will see how great our God is. This desire is our response to what God first did for us, that even while we were His enemies, He first loved us. His great grace saved wretches like us and out of that love, so we desire to see others come to know that grace and out of that grace disciple others. "By this all people will know you are my disciples, if you have love for one another." (John 13:35)

To God be the glory!

CHAPTER

4

Developing Entry Points for Men

By Brian Doyle

There is a real and strong felt need inside every local church to have a ministry to men. Often this ministry is carried out with good intentions, but with less than good execution. Gathering men and engaging them to grow in Christ is very different than doing the same with women, youth, and children. Any local church leader would likely acknowledge this as fact, yet the execution of men's ministry often is not that different than what is done with women, youth, and children. This chapter is designed to create awareness of what is different and what the initial steps are to create entry points that consistently work in ministry to men.

The majority of men do not have a strong felt need to gather with other men, for a host of reasons: too busy, not a priority, they don't want others to know them, they are scared, etc. This reality is key to understanding the marketing and execution of entry points for men. Men are wired for mission and for significance. Often they will sift through an invitation to gather, through their own grid of time management. They may genuinely consider if attending this event is a good stewardship of limited time. They know that scriptures like Psalm 133:1, which says, how blessed it is when brothers dwell together in unity, but they don't really know what that means and they would rather be doing something else. Godly men who are others-centered and who are operating under the Lordship of Christ will carefully consider if gathering in any form with other men is a higher priority than investing time with their wife, their kids, their extended family, their responsibilities at work, their responsibilities at home; the list goes on and on. Understanding this at the start is very important if church leadership hopes to build a consistent ministry to men.

Each church must go beyond the felt need to just gather the men and get them connected to creating intentionality in ministry and in every entry point promoted to the men. The compelling ministry mission is to build into the men, but with others in mind. Men are wired by God to be relatively independent and the majority are not looking for the local church to care for them and nurture them. Very few churches have ever had the experience of men whining that there aren't more programs in the church for men. Men are rarely the squeaky wheel of the local church, but rather are the silent minority that is quite happy to be left alone. The result is that few churches have significant programs for men, a ministry budget for men comparable to other groups and a staff member shepherding men. The reason lies in the lack of a strong vision for men and how to intentionally create multiple entry points for men that will serve to encourage, establish and equip them as spiritual leaders.

Wide entry points for men often occur on a Saturday for most churches. This Saturday ministry must be radically different than the Sunday morning ministry men are accustomed to at their local church. Each entry point for men must be masculine by design and have purposes that cannot be accomplished in a mixed setting. Much of this chapter will give insight and examples of what this can and should look like in a typical local church.

The return of investment from an effective entry point will be most clearly seen in the missional communities that develop as a result. Relationships that are initiated and fostered as a result of the entry point are the long-term fruit of this part of the ministry to men. Building brotherhood can often be accomplished with simple adjustments to the planning of an event that makes connection and exceptional execution a higher priority than frequency and content. Every church's entry point for men must be made with excellence, not only to glorify God but also simply to attract and bless the men who attend. Men are not as likely to extend grace to others when it comes to events where they sacrifice their time to participate. Frequency is not nearly as important as excellence. Consequently, a men's ministry mantra could be: do less, do it better.

The commitment to the vision of building men with others in mind is critical to making an entry point for men a church priority. A men's ministry event can and should impact the wider body of Christ and beyond, as men grow in godliness and are equipped as servant leaders. Church leadership must give high visibility to an entry point for men to communicate to men and everyone else the importance of the men's event. Overcoming a man's low felt need for church sponsored entry points is one of several needs that will be referenced in this chapter.

Hallmark of Entry Points

Your church-based entry points for men should have three goals: relationships, relevance, and return. Run the planning and execution of your entry points through these clear goals and the effectiveness of your entry point will rise very quickly.

Relationships

Years ago, our church took 90 men to a men's conference in New York. We worked hard to give every man a personal touch and although recruiting men was still a challenge, we reached a critical mass of the men of the church. Many men, in addition to the group from our church, attended the conference and that really impacted our men. We felt like we were part of something. The question is—what were we part of?

That summer, over half of the men accepted an invitation to be part of a small group. This was great and we knew that it would be in small groups where men would grow and change. People (including men) change in the context of relationships and a high percentage of the men in our church did not have a significant relationship with any other man. This is actually pretty normal. That same year a national survey stated that among the men who attended the conference, only 5% of these men had what they would describe as a "best friend." They knew what a best friend looked like because they had a friend like this in the military, in their college fraternity, on a sports team or during their school days. But, they no longer had a man like that in their life.

The summer ended, the fall church season kicked in, and many of the men who had said yes to an invitation to be in a small group were now withdrawing from that involvement. As we headed into the New Year, only a minority of men who had attended the men's conference the previous year were now in a small men's group. *What happened?*

We had made some mistakes. One very clear mistake was how we put these small groups of men together. We had recruited some leaders and then put together the groups on the basis of convenience. We tried to make it easy for men to say yes to a small group, so we gathered men by:

- Day of the week
- Time of day
- Geographic location
- Book, topic or Bible study

This had positive short-term results but did not work for the long term. There were exceptions, but we had made the mistake of assuming that men would make a relational commitment to men that they really did not know. The conference was a big help in getting men acquainted with one another, but we needed to develop a variety of safe entry points where men could move from acquaintances to friends. As men were connected to one another at these events, they could then receive a personal invitation from an emerging friend who would invite them based on relationship and not because of convenience. Now when we invite men to be part of a small group we do six things:

- Invite them to be part of the start of a new small group
- Let them know the date or time has *not* been decided
- Let them know that the meeting location has *not* been decided
- Let them know that the book or topic has *not* been decided
- Affirm them as a friend
- Let them know when the group will end (give a clear exit point)

When we create an entry point for men, we now run the event through a grid of questions that include, "Will this event help men get to know one another so that they might accept an invitation to be part of a small group."

Remember that the first goal when putting on an entry-level event for men is relationships.

Relevance

It was at the same conference that another survey question produced an interesting answer. Men were asked to describe their local church experience on Sunday morning. Two words came up more than any others. These were two words from men who not only attend church but who also accepted an invitation to attend multi-day, out of state men's conference! What words would you use to describe your own Sunday morning experience in your own local church?

The two words from the men who were surveyed that came up most often were 1) boring and 2) irrelevant. Can you say, "Ouch!" How did this happen? How did the most visible entry point of a typical local church, which is pastored by men and has leadership primarily of men, end up becoming boring and irrelevant to men? What do men mean when they say that Sunday morning is boring and irrelevant? Let's start by looking at those two words:

- Boring—tiresome, tedious, dull
- Irrelevant—no bearing on the matter at hand

It should be noted that these men were not thinking of the overall ministry of the church, but only of the Sunday morning worship service. A caring Christ-like community that is mission-minded and is God's representative on this earth is neither boring nor irrelevant.

We have already stated that Sunday morning is not the prime entry point for men to come into the local church. It is not my intention in this chapter or our intention in this book to take on the redevelopment of the Sunday morning service. What I will encourage is that we need to intentionally develop entry points for men outside of the Sunday morning worship service that are absolutely 1) interesting and 2) relevant to men.

What would be interesting and relevant to adult men? Let's start by defining the terms:

- Interesting—exciting the curiosity and holding the attention
- Relevant—bearing to the matter at hand, pertinent, timely

The last few years I have had the opportunity to present fathering seminars at dozens of local churches all over the country. These in-house seminars equip men to be great fathers and great grandfathers. Why have these seminars been so successful? I believe it is because they are interesting and relevant. Men already want to be great dads! These seminars engage a man's heart as well as his mind. They hold a man's attention because they engage him in an area of life that is very, very important to him. These seminars are specific, practical and applications can be put into practice immediately.

When you plan an entry-level event for men, you must consider if it will excite the typical man's curiosity as well as being timely and pertinent for the average man at your church. If it is content driven, will the content address an area relevant to the life of an adult man? If it is not content driven, will the event engage men in an area of current interest?

Remember that the second goal when putting on an entry-level event for men is relevance.

Return

Leaders ask the question when addressing how to create momentum in your church-based men's ministry, "How do you overcome the inertia in men?" Many men in the local church are not moving forward in their spiritual life. Our significant challenge is to help them move from their prolonged state of rest to ongoing growth and change.

Pastors and leaders around the country have worked hard at men's ministry over the years. This has especially been true as the visibility of men's ministry has risen. What are the results of this hard work? Although there are exceptions, the results have typically been a series of starts and stops. Churches experience a short season of success followed by an even longer season of failure. They see men come out to an event or a conference or a series of seminars, but are not able to keep the interest of the men. We might call this "creating momentum without capturing and sustaining the momentum."

The starts and stops in ministry to men may be due to disconnected entry points, bad timing, poor quality, poor leadership and a host of other reasons. A common reason is a lack of attention to the potential return that an event will bring to the ministry. If you are willing to work hard to put on a first-class, entry-level event for men, then you want to make sure that there is a tangible return for your work. This is just good stewardship!

This return can and should look different for different events. Some examples might include:

Event	Return
Attending a baseball game	50% of men succeed in bringing a guest
Fathering seminar	Dads begin to read the Bible to their children
Men's breakfast	Men who attend will come to the next breakfast
Serving projects	Multiple men serving together
Sunday school class	Men commit to pray once a week for other men
Men's conference	Four-week follow up for the men who attend
Four-week follow-up	2 out of 3 men accept an invitation to a small group

Developing entry points that work for men is just too difficult not to give focused attention to a planned and prayerful return on investment. How does the event fit into your men's ministry calendar? Will it launch what you are planning next for the men? Is there a specific result that can come out of the event? Will the visibility and reputation of the men's ministry be enhanced because of this event? Will new men come to know the Lord or the church or one another because they attended this event?

Remember that the third goal when putting on an entry-level event for men is return.

Distinctively Masculine

Your church-based entry point for men should always be distinctively masculine. A men's event should not just be a church sponsored event where only men attend. The planning and preparation should make sure that the event is distinctively masculine. Here are a few ideas to help that happen.

Make it Men Only

It is tough to pull off an event that is distinctively masculine when both men and women attend. I was asked to speak at a regional men's event a number of years ago and was surprised at who attended the well-publicized men's summit. I arrived early and connected with a couple of friends who were hosting the event at their church. It looked very organized and they were expecting a good crowd. As I spoke to the sound engineer, I realized that there were quite a large number of women around the church. I commented that it was very nice of the women to volunteer and support the men's event. He shared that actually some of the women had asked if they could attend the event and the leadership had said it would be alright. I pointed out to him that the program of the day specified men's summit. He hedged a little, but his reply was that the leadership had opened up the event to men and women. We had a good half day together but there was very little distinctly masculine about our time together. The worship was sweet, the hall was pretty, and I had to change my message.

Most women understand that there is a time and a place for men to come together. They know the special dynamic that exists when sisters in Christ gather and they recognize that a similar dynamic is true when brothers in Christ gather. There is no secret agenda and men are not conspiring to take over anything. We just want to hear from God and sharpen one another so that we can become His man.

At the Iron Sharpens Iron Men's Conferences, we have a simple rule: no women in the meeting rooms. There are women helping, serving, and administrating many aspects of the conference but they are not in the sanctuary or in the equipping seminars. They are at the registration table, in the exhibit hall and showing hospitality with refreshments. They bring much-needed warmth to the conference experience. We also have several conference sites where women volunteer to intercede in prayer for the men on-site at the conference. They huddle up in a room away from the men and the conference leadership encourages the attendees to fill out a 3" x 5" index card with a current and anonymous prayer request. These cards are passed on to the women gathering in prayer and they take the men to the throne of grace. That is pretty awesome.

Make the Content Specific to Men

The reason I had to change my message that day is because it can be inappropriate to teach on some topics in a mixed setting. In 2001, our ministry surveyed men across the Northeast and found that 63% of men claim that sexual temptation was their number one temptation. This is an example of a topic that is distinctively masculine. It is inappropriate to try having a meaningful teaching or training on sexual temptation in a mixed setting. It is also inappropriate to have a series men's gathering and not bring up a man's number one temptation. I have regularly seen men confess sin and cry out to God in repentance when content specific to men is addressed in a masculine environment.

Although addressing strongholds like sexual temptation and destructive anger are examples of content that is specific to men, there are many other topics that resonate with men and several that can only be addressed in a men's gathering.

In May of 2016, the Iron Sharpens Iron Network of Conference Ministries asked thousands of men if their own local church had ever offered any kind of seminar or teaching specific to being a father. The results were that less than 1 in 5 churches had offered this recently and more than 60% had not offered something like this ever in their memory. Training men about the unique role of being a dad is different than training men and women about the importance of parenting.

This would be similar to teaching and training married men in their role as husbands. A man more easily receives the ownership of the content when it is specific to them. Few local churches do well in engaging men in areas that God has called them to rise up. The typical man feels like his life is very full and unless the content or the calling is specific to him as a man, then he may well allow someone else to step in and cover the need. As our culture grows increasingly gender neutral, it will become increasingly significant to gather men together and teach them with content that is specific to them.

Make the Setting Safe for Men

David Murrow, of ChurchForMen.com, describes how the church sanctuary can be less than masculine in appearance. Flowers, wall art, robes, and colors can create a setting that does not stir the spirit of a man. This is especially true for the man who is new to the Sunday morning church experience. He knows intuitively that the facility was not designed with him in mind and he is a guest at something that was created for women. Without intent, a man has his guard up in this environment and thus is less likely to connect to God and respond to the message.

In the 1990's, Promise Keepers showed us that men worship differently, connect to other men differently and respond to God differently when the event takes place outside of the church. A man shows up at a football stadium or basketball arena wearing a polo shirt and a ball cap. He picks up a pretzel and soda and finds a seat in section 221. He knows this place as he comes here to watch the local team a couple of times a year. He stretches out and waits for things to get started. His guard is down and he brings all of his masculinity with him into this place.

Note that a men's event can be distinctively masculine inside the church. Every Iron Sharpens Iron Men's Conference takes place inside a local church. Flowers may be moved and some adjustments are made, but the setting can become male friendly. It may be helpful for your own entry points for men to move your event into the fellowship hall or the gym and out of the sanctuary. The very simple goal is to do whatever is needed to help a man bring all of his masculinity with him when he attends the event.

We know "God created man in his own image, in the image of God he created him, male and female he created them" (Gen 1:27). Men and women are different and a masculine context is different than a feminine context. Let's consider several elements of a masculine context that may give additional insight into adjustments we can make in our ministry to men.

Masculine Context #1: Men Tend to View Distance as Safety. Most men need their space. Women often feel better by talking about their issues, while a man feels better by simply solving problems. He does that by distancing himself and by going into his cave to give himself time to process. A man goes into his cave for three reasons:

- He needs to think about a problem and find a practical solution
- He doesn't have an answer to a question or problem
- He has become upset or stressed and needs to be alone

Suggestion: Give men space when setting up a room for your event. Do not set up chairs so men feel like they are on top of the other men.

Masculine Context #2: Men Tend to be Problem Solvers. Most men are problem solvers. They tend to value power, competency, efficiency and achievement highly. Problem-solving is a way of demonstrating these attributes. Men want to get to the bottom line.

- Men communicate primarily with facts
- Men want to get the core issue quickly and directly
- Men want to tackle the issue and solve it

Suggestion: Gather men together periodically with an issue that does not have a clear answer and white board their thinking to stimulate their creativity and determination in problem-solving.

Masculine Context #3: Most Men are Goal Oriented. Achieving goals is very important to men because it is a way for them to feel good about themselves. The more they achieve without anyone helping them, the better they feel about themselves. Autonomy is the symbol of efficiency, power, and control.

- Men need to be challenged
- Men need a clear goal
- Men need to achieve the goal

Suggestion: Ask men for counsel and contribution for larger than life, city-wide initiatives that clearly have a huge impact.

Masculine Context #4: Most Men have Tunnel Vision. Most men can manage one thing at a time. Different subjects and relationships are kept in different compartments and need to be managed individually.

- Men need to know the clearly defined goals
- Men need action steps
- Men need to see now what they should do now

Suggestion: Build a theme for your men's ministry, but offer men one option at a time and not a clutter of different initiatives. Find creative ways of offering the same thing.

Masculine Context #5: Most Men Tend to Value Rules over Relationships. Men want structure and want their questions answered. They need to understand expectations and these expectations should make sense. They also want a certain flexibility with this structure and not just a military environment. Too much structure will shut men down and squash their engagement.

- Men need structure to bring about order
- Too much structure (rigidity) will repel the men
- The goal of structure is to develop a non-threatening environment

Suggestion: Encourage a discipleship initiative for men church-wide that is a single issue and has clarity in both goals and objectives.

Masculine Context #6: Most Men Express Emotion in the Form of Anger. Men tend to be all or nothing in expressing their emotions. They show anger or nothing, as anger is the primary emotion for the majority of men. Emotions other than anger are only expressed in safe, ongoing relationships that allow time for them to surface.

- Men need to learn how to handle destructive anger
- Men need a safe place to express their anger
- Men need time to process their anger

Suggestion: Initiate one-on-one mentoring relationships with the men of the church to create safe zones where men can be honest and open regarding their struggles.

Ministry to men should look different and feel different than the ongoing Sunday morning ministry of the local church. It should attract men with distinctives that help them feel comfortable and valued.

Key Principles

If your church has had an up and down history with ministry to men, then you are like most every local church. Less than 10% of churches have a consistent fruitful ministry to men. Some of this is a result of simply not being aware of some key principles when building entry points for men. Here are several that bear special attention.

Do Less. When I first started to coach churches in developing entry points for men, I would urge them to create a monthly entry point and build this so that it was always in front of the men, women, and youth of the church. This would keep ministry to men front and center throughout the year and allow any visiting man to clearly see when and where he can connect with the men of the church. The principles here are solid but most men's leaders discover that 30 days go by very quickly and without significant help from church staff, the monthly entry point is likely too much. The answer is simply to do less and this typically means every other month or once a quarter.

Do it Better. Men's ministry leaders quickly come to understand that although men are saved by grace, they often do not extend much grace. One reason a quarterly entry point is usually more effective than a monthly entry point is because there is additional time to nail the details of the event and make sure that it is excellent in every way. Men value excellence and choose whether to invest their time and energy based on a history of performance excellence.

Start on Time and End on Time. An important part of making an entry point well is to be very intentional to start on time and to end on time. The men's entry point is an extra commitment for most men and they are carving time out of their schedule to attend. Be careful to promote the start and end times and then be faithful to follow through with them, as men will plan the balance of their day based on what you have communicated to them. Do not delay your start until more men arrive and do not extend your end until everything has been accomplished. As an example, the Iron Sharpens Iron Conferences are promoted as 8:30 AM - 4:55 PM so that men know that the conference leadership is committed to ending on time.

Personal Invitation. Another reason a quarterly or every other month is effective is because the men's ministry team needs time to promote and to extend personal invitations to each man in the church. If the men's ministry has a high-profile monthly event, then either the men's leadership team is seemingly inviting men almost every week to an event or the men's team stops making personal invitations. Neither of these is good. Men not only need to know about an entry point, but they also need to know that they are wanted and who specifically wants them to be there. The goal for any local church of any size is that every man gets a personal invite to each and every entry point for men.

Rhythm. Whether a church has a monthly, bi-monthly or quarterly men's entry point event is not nearly as important as creating a rhythm for the men's ministry. A significant purpose of the entry point is the ongoing visibility it gives to everyone about the men's ministry of the church. All people need to know that ministry to men is a priority. The men need to know the when and how often so that they can adjust their work and personal calendars to accommodate this entry point. Developing a trustworthy rhythm is an important feature in building an effective entry point.

Pastoral Support. In most local churches, the senior pastor is a man and the people of the church want to know how important the pastor considers the men's ministry entry point. They will look to see if he champions it from the platform on Sunday morning and they will look to see if he attends it with the other men of the church. The most effective churches have a pastor who exhorts the men of the church to join him and gives them reasons to attend.

All Men Invited. There are cases where a men's ministry event that was created as an entry point for all the men of the church and their friends has, over time, become a club where the same men come every time. All men should, first off, include the younger men, age 13 and older. This means the youth ministry needs to be sensitive to the schedule of the men's ministry and not offer young men anything on that same day. All men also means that the wide breadth of the men around the church are truly welcome at the entry point.

Gathering Men. We know that the entry point needs promotion from the platform on Sunday morning in front of everyone and we know men need a personal invitation to know that they are wanted. Men also need to know who is coming. We suggest creating a sign-up board and not using a sign-up sheet. The principle is that the sign-up board placed in the church foyer or fellowship hall or in some prominent place lets everyone know who is coming to the event and who is not. The leadership team should have certain names already on the board before setting it up. Place it is in a strategic spot so that everyone sees it every Sunday.

Worship. There may be an opportunity to have worship at your men's event. Many things need to happen for this to enhance the masculine context you are trusting God to create. This would include a critical mass of men, a team of gifted musicians and choosing songs that clearly work for men. If there is a question on any of these, then it may be wise not to have praise worship and singing.

Saturday, not Sunday. One reason it is not necessary to have praise worship and singing is because your typical large entry point for men is on a Saturday and not a Sunday. Your Saturday event should be very different than a Sunday morning church service. The content, the format, the flow should be planned to be purposefully different and intentionally masculine.

Exhortation. Another difference between Sunday morning ministry and your entry point for men is that this might be an appropriate time to exhort the men. A men's event setting is much safer for men than the church service. They are more likely to lower their guard and receive a challenge directed at the crowd of men from another man. Men need to hear strong biblical exhortation, but it needs to be in the right setting. The best exhortation contains an element of modeling such as when Joshua exhorted the men of Israel "… choose this day whom you will serve, ... but as for me and my house we will serve the Lord." (Joshua 24:15)

Transparency and Vulnerability. Few teaching pastors are transparent and vulnerable in their regular teaching ministry. It is not usually the right setting to be open and transparent especially as it relates to failure, temptation, and sin. The men's event is the place where men need to hear from other men who have the same struggles, temptation and failures yet can model how to be an overcomer and find victory in Christ. At the core of why men are not growing aggressively in Christ is a lack of honesty in friendships. Your speakers need to model transparency and vulnerability.

Heart and Not Just Head. A major reason for the need to select gifted speakers who are open, honest, transparent, and vulnerable is because a goal of your men's event is to engage a man's heart and not just his head. Information is good but inspiration must be part of your regular entry point for men. This type of challenging inspiration point men to Christ and challenges them to yield all things to His Lordship.

Critical Mass. This has been mentioned previously and it is critical to any entry point for men. You must fill the room, as that is what creates critical mass. You do not need hundreds of men, but the room you choose for your entry point needs to be near capacity. This is part of creating a safe zone for men. They see that a critical mass of men showed up. Use tables and chairs to fill your room creatively and choose your facility wisely.

Callin' Men Out

Periodically, God calls men out. He instructed Moses to call men out three times each and every year. These three times were entry points for the men of Israel. Moses did this to celebrate the three feasts that were special occasions. Each of these three feasts occurred on an annual basis. There was a rhythm to these events. Many other things happened in men's lives between these feasts—but three times a year every man was required to set aside what they were doing and gather with the much larger nation of men and appear before the Lord. This was critical mass and God Himself, through Moses, called the men out. There is no greater champion than Almighty God for a men's event. Let's look at the scriptures that mandated these entry points for men:

> Exodus 23:17 "Three times a year all your males shall appear before the Lord GOD." (NASB)

> Exodus 34:23 "Three times a year all your males are to appear before the Lord GOD, the God of Israel." (NASB)

> Deuteronomy 16:16 "Three times in a year all your males shall appear before the LORD your God in the place which He chooses." (NASB)

One typical reason that the men of your church may decline an invitation to a men's only event is that they have a family and are hesitant to use their discretionary time by attending something that pulls them away from their wife and kids. God dealt with this issue with the Hebrews by commanding them to gather with other men. You might be wondering if it was really a top priority that the Hebrew men leave their wife, their kids, the sick and the elderly. Who would protect these loved ones from their very real enemies in the surrounding lands while the men were away? The answer is that the Lord Himself would care for them. In fact, the Lord stated that He would see to it that no one would even be interested or even think about attacking them during the three times each year that He called the men together. Note verse 24 of chapter 34:

> Exodus 34:23-24 "Three times a year all your males are to appear before the Lord God, the God of Israel. For I will drive out nations before you and enlarge your borders, and no man shall covet your land when you go up three times a year to appear before the Lord your God." (NASB)

Here is a question for you to ponder: when was the last time, if ever, that someone called you out to join with every other man and appear before the Lord? Who even has the posture to make that type of call out in your own local church?

There are no commands in Scripture for New Testament Christian men to gather like this from my studying of the Bible. We are free from this mandate like many other Old Testament laws and ordinances. Do you think though that some of the principles of this Old Testament command are consistent with God's design for Christian men in the 21st Century?

As we close, this chapter here is something to consider. What can you and a couple brothers in Christ from your own local church do to initiate a new entry point for the men of your church? In addition, what can you do to gather with men from other churches and do together what you may not be able to do alone? There is also likely an annual Iron Sharpens Iron Men's Conference in your region. Conferences like ISI are only once per year but they are an opportunity to gather as men of God and to be part of something bigger than ourselves and experience the fellowship of the larger church. What do you think?

Has the Almighty God wired us to benefit from this? If so—let's get started!

CHAPTER
5

Developing Men's Small Groups

By Dave Enslow

There is Nothing Small about Men's Groups

This chapter deals with the rationale, process, and current methodology of developing what are commonly called small groups. Here, we have attempted to show the historical value of men leading others within groups, fill in some current knowledge gaps and point you to a few newer innovations in small group development for men. The key objective for groups is to develop an environment for friendships and deep bonds of brotherhood while growing and developing mature followers of Christ. The best ministries to men will recognize the necessity of a spiritual growth pathway and will offer a variety of groups that appeal to the various needs of men.

Whether you are activating new groups for men or looking for ways to reignite your group ministries, keep in mind there is nothing small about small groups. Groups are the best place for great spiritual growth when the dynamics of meeting with other men are fully understood.

Past philosophies and patterns have shaped the way small group ministries are handled as if one size fits all, but men are different.

In the Beginning

Are These Old Testament Small Groups?

Isn't it interesting that we often begin talking about developing small groups as if they are a 21st-century construct? It is useful to understand the basis for small groups, so before we delve into the practical points of small group development, let's take a look at the Biblical and historical development of the smallest of small groups.

The family and the principle of male headship are well established in the Garden of Eden. It is clear in the instructions given to Adam in the garden that God created man for relationships. God cared about man enough to give him dominion and the ability to tend all within the man's charge. As we move from creation, or generation, to degeneration (the fall) and onto regeneration, we see that God was bringing his people together into a deeper relationship with each other and himself. The Almighty continues to show us there are only the people of God and those who are not. He carefully orchestrates seemingly disconnected events to be certain that the family of God will grow through grace and mercy as they live in the midst of a sinful people.

In Genesis 6: 5-6 (NASB) it says that "...the LORD saw that the wickedness of man was great on the earth, and that every intent of the thoughts of his heart was only evil continually. The LORD was sorry that He had made man on the earth, and He was grieved in His heart." The story of Noah and his seven family members is well known; they are brought into the physical protection of the Ark through the divine protection of God. This particular family ministry, once again, is led by the spiritual head, in this case, Noah. As time continues, some of the sons will lead their families well and some will not.

I don't want to paint a picture here with anything other than broad brushstrokes. I would not want to insert something into the scriptures which is not there. I believe, however, we may see that even though God never calls these people into "small groups," he does label them as tribes. He brings people together in relationships that will help them grow and develop personally and bring Glory to himself. This will be an important premise to remember as we unpack the best practices in developing small groups later in this chapter.

God has designed men to lead, and he often sends someone to the leader for support and midcourse corrections. Moses' father-in-law is a good example of this. Jethro instructed Moses in a technique many have called the Jethro principle, found in Exodus 18. Jethro tells Moses to select capable men "from all the people" and appoint them over thousands, hundreds, fifties, and tens. In summary, he basically tells him that doing this will please God and himself. If he doesn't take his advice, he's going to wear himself out. This is a key principle to remember when groups begin to multiply, as we will see later.

As the pages of Biblical history turn to the New Testament, we hear from John and his proclamation that it's going to be a new day with God. There is one coming who is going to bring about changes and no one can even imagine what this will mean. Today, we have become quite accustomed to Jesus' selection of the twelve. He handpicked some men and changed a couple of their names and then he spent every day with them until he went to the cross (Mark 3). These new disciples experienced the transforming power of living life together with Christ. This movement of men became known as The Way. What happened to and through The Way cannot be underestimated as we begin to see how Jesus used a small group of men to change the world forever.

In the book of Acts, we witness the culmination of the years of training Jesus gave his disciples. His training is most often experienced as they go through the years of Jesus' ministry with Him. Being with Him and being together is another important key when we move from individuals coming to Christ, to becoming a follower of Christ. If we are not leading men to live life in Him, with Him and through Him, we have left them to be baby believers without the necessary care to develop into biblical manhood.

For these few men in the first century, there is a new empowerment, a flash point in the history of God's men moving out, and then into every area of their culture. We see a complete renewal of this motley, small group after the coming of the Holy Spirit. The Scriptures tell us in Acts 2:42 -47 and 4:32-37 that 3,000 were transformed as the gospel was proclaimed. They devoted themselves to the breaking of bread, prayer, and the sharing of anything necessary as they met together. The Lord added to their groups every day. Their lives were built into one another and there was a bond of brotherhood that encouraged everyone.

As the book of Acts closes and Paul completes his missionary journeys, Luke leaves us with a kind of open-ended closure. This is a bit puzzling and not what many of us want when we come to the end of a story. A few commentators have suggested that this is because the story continues. You and I carry on the mission of those who were sent forth.

Here We Are—Now What?

The early disciples began a firestorm of controversy along with the growth of a new movement. These men were labeled variously and often derogatorily. The people of The Way were called Christ-ins and suffered greatly, even to death, for their new found faith. In the first 400 years after Jesus rose to life, the Christian faith spread to most of the cities of the Roman Empire.

My hope as we continue to explore how these groups of men developed is that we see the God of history allowing his church to unfold and grow from Acts all the way to this present time, regardless of what we are called or how we are treated. God has marked us out to continue a movement of men who will lead his people, the church, until the triumphant return of Christ.

From the book of Acts to the time of the 16th-century Protestant reformation, history tells of a church that is militant. Disagreements, strife, councils, and schisms that occurred, but did not thwart God's advancement of his men and His Kingdom purpose. In fact, it appears that the church in the world tends to grow through a kind of continuing cellular division. This will be helpful to understand as we continue to examine how this new expression of Christ's Church develops and morphs into something quite different than its beginnings.

Our focus on developing small groups for men is better understood when we see that God has gathered larger numbers of people to Himself by allowing developments like the Gutenberg Bible. This single breakthrough places His word in the hands of the common man. From this time forward, the ability for someone to have a Bible, which might be shared with a small group of people, is no less than revolutionary to a church which has gathered large groups of people in one place in the past.

As literacy expanded through these years, ordinary people found that they could come together to hear someone read the Bible without being in a church building. Interestingly, the early church met this way to begin with and moved from private homes to larger synagogues. A few versions of the Bible came into use when it became evident that ordinary people were now able to access the Bible. King James I, of England, then produced an "official" Bible. As the education acts developed, more and more ordinary people became literate through the 1850's and Bibles became a household item.

From the Nineteenth Century to the Jesus Movement

It would be next to impossible to miss that men were drawing lines of division socially and culturally, even as Christian brothers, which culminated in a war between the states. Nevertheless, God has always shown us that in these times of great unrest, war, and death, they culminate in drawing households together often including people who are not biologically related. A cultural shift occurred that has affected us to this day.   From the reconstruction period to the Great Depression to the first and second World Wars, believers find strength and security meeting in churches and attending Sunday School.

The 1950's seemed like a time when almost everyone was a believer because the entire country was closed on Sunday. Pietism was a big deal, but there was unrest in many families. Through the Civil Rights Movement, assassinations, and the Vietnam war, this generation found themselves culturally divided. Now there are gatherings called support groups, a movement built from the groundswell of unrest and dispute over social issues called the Jesus movement. High school and college campuses around the country teaming with Jesus freaks as Bible clubs developed outside the church buildings. Young Christians were found in strange places like boardwalks at ocean beaches, passing out tracts, meeting in small coffee houses and singing new praises to Jesus in community centers on weeknights. It seemed to some that this was a return to the first-century church, as young men and women even decided to live in communal groups.

Iron John and the Men of the 90's

Men became confused by the unisex movement as some followed a secular call to restore themselves to whom they truly are. This secular movement of men found itself colliding with Christian men, Bible believers, and the need to be with other men was acknowledged by all. In this era, a growing number of men found that "group" is a place to go. Now, all of the issues that affect men are coming together as they began to express themselves openly. The Bible was less to be studied as it was lived. Postmodern questions were no longer dismissed but grappled with as men met to find the true meaning of manhood— Biblical manhood. Much is written and told of the Promise Keepers movement and those great days of stadiums full of men singing praises to Jesus, locking arms in solidarity with other men from various backgrounds and promising to live as better husbands, fathers, and sons. What is not immediately apparent is the far-reaching impact this movement had upon men in this the 21st century.

Developing the Right Next Step for Your Men's Group

We have taken a backward look to the smallest of small groups from the very beginning and progressed to our present times. This will help us understand that God has been urging his men to be leaders of households and to band together with other men forever. As we said before, some men do this well and some do not. To be sure the basics have been the same, God will lead us and we will be his people. (2 Co 6:16, Ezra 37:27).

Whether the gathering of people is called households, families, tribes or small groups, we have seen they are consistent with the growth of the people of God, the church. The writer of Hebrews even gives us the imperative for meeting with one another in Hebrews 10:25 (NASB), "...not forsaking our own assembling together, as is the habit of some, but encouraging one another; and all the more as you see the day drawing near.

For Your Team: New and Improved

Probably the worst two words in modern marketing have been, "new and improved." Since there is nothing new about meeting together in groups, what can be improved? The message of the Bible is the same today as it always has been; however, delivery systems have made some changes over time. Take a look at our current Christ-following world in America and we can see that technology and the advancements therein could easily become distractions, if not the actual reason for not meeting together. If one is asking why we need to meet together with other men, leaders of men must have an answer. There is simply no replacement for time spent together, but today this has become the goal rather than the starting point for most men.

"Think big, start small, go deep." Dawson Trotman, founder of The Navigators, used this slogan to fuel a discipleship movement. We may add to it, along with the Apostle Paul, saying, "and finish well." If we are to reach men in an intentional discipleship movement, a strategy not unlike that of Jesus' needs to be followed. No matter what new and improved curricula have been developed, a strategy through which it will be used is most important.

Before grabbing that great new book or the latest video series for men, start with a small team of men for developing groups. If you do not have a men's team at all, *stop* right here and check out the chapter on building a men's ministry team. Take stock of some men around you; look for a man who is already leading a group. Once you have established this team, be certain that men's groups are non-negotiable. You must, as we have seen Biblically and historically, have men meeting in groups. Your small group team is in itself, a men's group. Don't miss this important step by making it a business meeting. Your team will be the first flash point for all future men's groups. It should *not* become a governing board.

Asking questions like, "What do we expect of each other" and "What do we expect from the men in our church," will help you as you continually shape the pathway along which you and your men will develop.

Here is a list that a team of men uses to remind them why their men's groups exist and the Christ-like character qualities we gain when men are sharpening men:

Well thought of by outsiders
Dignified
Not double-tongued
Not addicted to much wine
Not greedy for dishonest gain
A confident believer
Not arrogant
Not quick tempered

Hospitable
A lover of good
Upright
Holy
Disciplined
Able to instruct in the word
Above reproach
The husband of one wife
Sober-minded
Self-controlled
Respectable
Hospitable
Able to teach
Not a drunkard
Not violent, but gentle
Not quarrelsome
Not a lover of money
A good household manager
An effective father
A mature believer

Notice these are not new definitions of manhood. They are derived from the leadership requirements found in 1 Timothy: 3. If our men's groups are about anything useful, they must be about developing men into the leaders God has called them to be.

The primary principle is to think of your curriculum as the scaffolding around a building. Curricula, no matter how complete or highly polished, should not take the place of building into men in a variety of ways. Do not get stuck here. Curricula can be replaced without much work. Conversations in your groups should eventually surpass reciting the answers to the fill-in-the-blank questions. Building into each other's lives takes time and may involve multiple group experiences for a man.

Where are the men? This is probably a question you ask or are being asked all the time. The first place to look is the church database. Even if it is archaic, in your mind, this data will be useful for developing men's groups. Your small group team should have a pretty good idea of who exists in the male population of your church. This will include their family relationship as well. If your data is sketchy or not reliable, work with the keeper of the data in your church and bring that person, male or female, into your men's group development stage. If you have an up to date system, be sure one of your small group team leaders is gaining a working knowledge of the system.

Review your lists of men, their ages, stage of life, where they live and work, and marital status. All this will help develop a good starting point for your group's pathway. Begin with the question, "Who do we want to reach?" rather than just striking out with a study for men expecting this to attract a variety of guys.

Intergenerational groups may work when identified as such. Think back to the subculture for a minute. If you want to connect with Gen X, Y, Z or now gen C, someone has to be or willing to become the expert within these groups. Think like a missionary to men. Yes, they are all men, but some are 13 to 15 years old living in a world where videos cannot last more than 6 seconds and others may be age 16-19 and think differently from their younger brothers. From this example, you can see how a team will expand and new segments of the men you want to move into groups grow and develop.

Cast a vision. What is the desired outcome? Too many ministries to men have become directionless men's clubs. If you need a reminder of why we are developing groups, read Matthew 28:18-20 (NASB), "All authority has been given to Me in heaven and on earth. Go therefore and make disciples of all the nations, baptizing them in the name of the Father and the Son and the Holy Spirit, teaching them to observe all that I commanded you; and lo, I am with you always, even to the end of the age." This is about making disciples, end of discussion.

Depending on the condition of your ministry men you may need to tailor your strategies accordingly. For instance, let's say you have some men already meeting regularly in a Bible study or prayer group and this has become the visible ministry to men. Do not shut this down and begin anew. These men could very well be the allies and assets to help you move men along in their spiritual growth. Place their group on a charted continuum, including some of the details about these men as we mentioned before. Ages, stage of life, the day they meet, personal interests, all help define the type of group these men are in. Even prayer groups pray differently. Put this in writing so your team is aware of what exists, where they meet, and who they may send a man to when asked.

As your men's group network develops, you will eventually find the budding leaders. Be sure you are documenting all this and intentionally asking them to lead a group in the future. Asking these men if they would be willing to take on the *task* of leading a group is a mistake. This is not a task; it is the commission of Christ. Every man needs to be reminded that, God is giving us an *opportunity* to lead other men.

Herding Cats or Discipling Men?

Many leaders get to the point where they feel like they are herding cats. Men are moving in multiple directions without any real signs of spiritual and often practical growth. With your developing leaders and a well-charted course of action for the year on paper, you will need a mechanism to move men into groups intentionally. The most overrated methods have been the pulpit announcement, the bulletin blurb and a sign-up sheet in the lobby. We will now look out a few ways to break this cycle.

Give men a way into a group. If you are a sports fan and you like attending a game once in a while, there is probably nothing better than a guy asking you to join him. A personal invitation to join a group of guys is the key to assimilation. If a man already knows one man, it will be a lot easier to get acquainted with some others in the group. Sign-up sheets or online forms should always be considered a way of recording data, *not* the way to get men into your groups.

An event that invites men to hang out together, have a meal, and perhaps listen to a speaker, will be the place you capture the attention of the men and move them into a group. Never miss this opportunity. It can be a golf outing, a beast feast or a breakfast, just don't stop with the event. Right then, at the end of the event, while they are in still seated, say something like this:

"Men, this was a great time tonight, wasn't it? I think we miss out when we avoid hanging out with each other, so we've planned a little extension of this time together. There are (you have chosen how many beforehand) three different opportunities to meet with some guys during the next few weeks. George over at this table will be going through the book (you already chose the book title just announce it) at Starbucks on Tuesday from 6:30 am until 7:30 am so you can meet and get off to work. Bob will be meeting at the church during the Wednesday night family night where they have child care, using the Gospel of John, and Pastor Bill will meet at his house Saturday at 9 am for a discussion about recovering Biblical manhood. Each of these groups will meet for just 4 weeks. So pick the time and place that will fit your schedule and move to the table where your man is sitting."

If no one moves, don't be surprised. You will just have to say—"Yes, it's time to move now."

The reason this will become the most effective way to get men into small groups is because it is active. This is the call to action that men need. During your vision casting, it will be helpful to remind the rest of the team that the goal of all events and activities is to move men into groups. One very effective way is to plan events with the right next steps built into the event. Have materials already included and available at the event.

Build camaraderie and brotherhood along the way. At any point after the men have been meeting, plan a time for a meal out together. It won't matter which meal it is; however, this is an opportunity for the group to work out the time and place together. The leader will direct but not make the final decision. This planning builds camaraderie and the meal continues to build up fellowship and brotherhood. Warning to the leader, do not create an agenda for this. Let the organic friendships develop naturally.

Give men a way out of a group. The reason we suggest four weeks in a previous illustration is to keep the exit ramp in sight. After three meetings the leader can say, "This is pretty good, don't you think? How about meeting for four more weeks after this?" This is an especially good mechanism for men who are not accustomed to meeting in a group. For all your groups, however, keep them to 8-13 weeks, maximum. A man who isn't fitting in with his group well needs to know there will be a different group he may meet with in the future.

Provide a break. After the group has been meeting for the scheduled time, say 13 weeks, take a break. This concept, based on the agricultural principle found in Exodus 23:11 (NASB), "...on the seventh year you shall let it rest and lie fallow...," provides an off ramp for a man to exit a group and process his experience. During this break of several weeks, men will often begin asking, "When will we meet again."

This break time is good for leaders to consider their role and to begin recruiting other men to lead. When the next group is announced for this time slot, it will be a new group. This will allow you to invite men to a group without them feeling like they are joining men who already meet.

Find a need, serve a need. In your discovery of who the men are and where they may be in their stage of life, you will find men who are hurting at some level. When a man expresses a need or desire while in a group, he could very well be the man who needs to lead a group on this very topic. You have probably read or will read of entry points into the ministry to and through men. Remind your group leaders that these issues may not be a fit for the current group, but can be used as entry points for other men in the congregation. When running groups on a cycle as we have mentioned, these topical groups will have an opportunity to invite men for their particular need. Examples may be porn issues, struggles with finances, marriage issues, or fitness and health, and a myriad of other felt needs.

Reverse the flow. Many churches have a model of moving people from the sanctuary on Sunday to the Christian education class/Sunday school with the hope of them joining a small group. Let's think about this in reverse. Again, do not change what is in place with your church, simply add a different mode for the men. Here is a scenario: a group meets at a local restaurant or in a man's home. This is generally not a

Bible study, rather a topical discussion where Biblical truths are openly shared. In this environment, a neighbor or co-worker is invited to hang out with some men for about an hour before or after work. This very low-level group will often bring unchurched, unbelieving men into the acquaintance of Christian men. These friends and neighbors who have preconceived ideas of what Christian men are and how they behave will be guided to Christ well before they even attend a church. Consider this outreach type of men's group to be cutting edge and the possibilities are endless. One such group has a virtual meeting.

Finish Well

Discipleship has been lacking in our churches for a very long time. Many program oriented, community serving churches have looked back upon their work only to find a giant disconnect among the men. Many of the men who we talk to have never had a continuing connection with other men over the years. The result we are experiencing is a loss of masculine vitality in the greater church family.

When we apply the Biblical family dynamics and recognize that ministry to men affects entire households, communities and beyond, the term small group doesn't seem to fit at all when speaking of men. Men are agents of change. This is a big deal, and unless challenged Biblically, developing men's groups may seem like just another church program to them. Always challenge your men with the right next step for them, to avoid the men's Bible group or men's club mentality.

As you set out to ignite or reignite your men's group movement with your team, here are some questions you may begin with:

- Do most men in our church understand what it means to be a disciple and the importance of meeting with men?

- Have we clearly defined what Biblical manhood is for the men?
- Do we know what a disciple is and what a disciple does?
- Does our senior pastor believe that the men of the church are his greatest supporters and willing to carry out his vision?
- Are our men's leaders intentionally discipling men wherever they are involved?
- Do we see most of our men involved in spiritual growth *and* service?
- Are we reaching men of all ages (including young men age 13 and up)?
- Do the spiritually mature men willingly lead small groups of men?
- Do we have opportunities for men at all spiritual levels to engage with a group?
- Can we consider an outreach group?
- Have we surveyed the men to determine their spiritual/social needs?

You will serve your men well if you begin casting your vision for developing men's groups with a clear Biblically masculine mandate. Not every man is a macho man. Consider a study of King David to help establish the perspective of a godly warrior King, who writes poems and plays the harp. As your need to reach different men with differing interest expands, allow leadership to rise from your groups. In fact, constantly be encouraging men to take on the opportunity to lead a group.

Just a word here about accountability. Many men shrink back at the idea of having to answer for their actions. Numerous times men have shared the negative experiences they have had in groups where lists were kept to hold one another accountable. You may even want to play down the word accountability itself. Don't take this the wrong way; accountability is very important. However, men will be truly accountable when men have relationships as friends and brothers. The desire to share burdens develop within a safe group of men and accountability becomes very natural.

The greatest reward from developing groups of men is to be a part of God's plan to increase his church not only in numbers but in strength, the strength of a Christ-like character that is developed with men just as Jesus did with his small group of men.

SURVEYS AND SCORE SHEETS

Men's Ministry Leadership Survey

Check the statements below that best describe your men's ministry.

1. Purpose Statement

    ☐ 1.1 We do not have a purpose statement for men's ministry.
    ☐ 1.2 We have a stated but unwritten purpose statement.
    ☐ 1.3 We have activities, but not a ministry focus.
    ☐ 1.4 We have a developed purpose statement with ministry-focused activities.

2. Leadership

    ☐ 2.1 We do not have an identified men's ministry leadership team.
    ☐ 2.2 We have one or two men who provide leadership to our men's ministry.
    ☐ 2.3 We have developed a broad-based leadership team.

3. Study Groups

    ☐ 3.1 We currently do not have men meeting in study groups.
    ☐ 3.2 We have several study groups that are meeting regularly.
    ☐ 3.3 We have many study groups that are meeting regularly.

4. Relationships

☐ 4.1 We do not have accountability relationships developed among the men in our church.

☐ 4.2 We have sporadic development of relationships among men; there is little accountability.

☐ 4.3 We have seen strong, vital relationships develop among men in the church; there is high accountability.

5. Scheduled Activities

☐ 5.1 We have one or two men's ministry activities a year.

☐ 5.2 We have some regularly scheduled men's ministry activities each year.

☐ 5.3 We have planned men's ministry activities to encourage men to participate at various levels of interest.

6. Outreach

☐ 6.1 We are seeing little or no participation in our men's ministry.

☐ 6.2 We are seeing some involvement in our men's ministry.

☐ 6.3 We have a large number of men who are involved in our men's ministry and they are actively inviting others.

7. Impact on the Family

☐ 7.1 We have a few men leading some form of regular family devotions in their home.

☐ 7.2 We have many men who lead some form of regular family devotions in their home.

☐ 7.3 We have men helping other men lead some form of regular family devotions in their home.

8. Impact on the Church

☐ 8.1 We have a few men who are active and who are having an impact in the church.

☐ 8.2 We have a core group of men who are committed to the pastor and the ministry of the church.

☐ 8.3 We have a significant number of men actively supporting the pastor and involved in church ministry.[4]

9. Atmosphere at the Church (Select the one that most reflects the current atmosphere at your Church)

☐ 9.1 We have a church atmosphere that emphasizes loving God, building caring relationships, and healing from wounds.

☐ 9.2 We have a church atmosphere that promotes a male-friendly environment, which loves God and builds caring relationships.

☐ 9.3 We have a church atmosphere that balances a male friendly environment with a female-friendly environment.

☐ 9.4 We have a church atmosphere that uses masculine language in challenging men to follow Christ and walk with God.

Men's Ministry Climate Survey

Hello, men. In order for [Church Name] to develop a first class ministry for all our men, we need to have honest and candid feedback. Please read and respond to this simple three-page questionnaire by completing all thirty questions. Your participation will make a difference in the lives of men.

Demographics

---

1. Age ☐ 13-19 ☐ 20-29 ☐ 30-39 ☐ 40-49 ☐ 50-59 ☐ 60 +

2. Marriage ☐ Never has been married
☐ Was married and am now divorced
☐ Am presently married—first marriage
☐ Am presently married—married more than once

3. Children ☐ Presently have children living at home under age 13
Presently have children living at home between 13 and 18
Presently have children, who are living away from home
Presently have no children

4. Work week? ☐ <40hrs ☐ 40-45hrs ☐ 46-50hrs ☐ 51-55hrs 56-60hrs ☐ >60

Personal Development

5. How long at your present job ☐ < 1 yr ☐ 2-3 yrs ☐ 3-5 yrs ☐ 6-10 yrs ☐ >10 yrs

6. How would you measure your job satisfaction the past twelve months?

   ☐ Best year ever in my work life
   ☐ Very satisfying
   ☐ Satisfying
   ☐ Less than satisfying
   ☐ Anxious to move to different employment

7. How long as a Christian? ☐ < 1 yr ☐ 2-3 yrs ☐ 3-5 yrs ☐ 6-10 yrs ☐ >10 yrs

8. How would you measure your growth in Christ the last twelve months?

   ☐ Most growth ever in my life in Christ
   ☐ Solid growth—not standing still
   ☐ Standing still—no measurable growth
   ☐ Struggling to grow for a variety of reasons
   ☐ Doing very poorly and need help

9. Do you have another man who helps you keep accountable in your walk with Christ?

   ☐ Yes ☐ No

Identify with Christ

10. How often have you invited another man to join you for Sunday morning worship at your church during the past two years?

   ☐ Weekly   ☐ Monthly   ☐ 2-3 times/yr   ☐ Almost never
   ☐ Never

11. How often have you shared the Gospel message with another person during the past two years?

   ☐ Weekly   ☐ Monthly   ☐ 2-3 times/yr   ☐ Almost never
   ☐ Never

12. If you are married, how often have you invited your wife to pray with you during the last two years (Do not include thanksgiving for meals)?

   ☐ Weekly   ☐ Monthly   ☐ 2-3 times/yr   ☐ Almost never
   ☐ Never

13. If you have children at home, how often in the past two years have you purposely gathered the family together for Bible reading and prayer?

   ☐ Weekly   ☐ Monthly   ☐ 2-3 times/yr   ☐ Almost never
   ☐ Never

Issues Facing Men

14. How often do you come into contact with pornography?

    ☐ Daily ☐ 2-3 Week ☐ Weekly ☐ Monthly ☐ 2-3 times/yr
    ☐ Never

15. How often do you lose your temper?

    ☐ Daily ☐ 2-3 Week ☐ Weekly ☐ Monthly ☐ 2-3 times/yr
    ☐ Never

16. How often do you gamble (Lottery, casino, online)?

    ☐ Daily ☐ 2-3 Week ☐ Weekly ☐ Monthly ☐ 2-3 times/yr
    ☐ Never

17. How often do you consume alcohol?

    ☐ Daily ☐ 2-3 Week ☐ Weekly ☐ Monthly ☐ 2-3 times/yr
    ☐ Never

18. How much alcohol do you consume (One drink is defined as 12 ounces of beer, 5 ounces of wine, or one standard cocktail (1.5 ounces of 80-proof liquor)?

    ☐ Never   ☐ 1 monthly   ☐ 2-4 monthly
    ☐ 2-4 weekly   ☐ 5 weekly

19. How many drinks containing alcohol do you have on a typical day when you are drinking?

   ☐ 1   ☐ 1-2   ☐ 3-4   ☐ 5-6   ☐ >6

Ministry

20. What kind of Christian small group are you presently involved with (Check all that relate)?

   ☐ Not in a regular small group of any kind
   ☐ Once a month small group
   ☐ Weekly or bi-weekly group of men and women
   ☐ Weekly or bi-weekly group of men

21.   Are you more likely to:

   ☐ Read a Christian book
   ☐ Listen to a Christian CD
   ☐ Listen to Christian radio
   ☐ Watch a Christian video
   ☐ Watch Christian television
   ☐ Watch non-Christian videos
   ☐ Watch non-Christian television
   ☐ I do none of the above

22. Please rate your interest in the items below: 1 = lowest through 6 = highest (mark one for each item)

a. Men's Bible Study	1	2	3	4	5	6
b. Camping trip	1	2	3	4	5	6
c. Golf scramble	1	2	3	4	5	6

d. Monthly breakfast	1	2	3	4	5	6
e. Chili cook-off	1	2	3	4	5	6
f. Men Sunday school	1	2	3	4	5	6
g. Sporting event	1	2	3	4	5	6
h. Fishing trip	1	2	3	4	5	6
i. Annual retreat	1	2	3	4	5	6
j. Service project	1	2	3	4	5	6
k. Father child outing	1	2	3	4	5	6
l. Equipping seminar	1	2	3	4	5	6

Low ------------------------- High

23. If you were to attend a seminar for men in the coming months, which ones would be of interest to you? Please check the top three.

□ Furthering my career   □ Developing friendship with wife

□ Godly fathering   □ Deepening my marriage

□ Lust/sexual temptation   □ Becoming a great dad

□ Witnessing   □ Managing money/budgets

□ Discipleship/spiritual   □ Dealing with anger
growth

□ Rites of passage training   □ Other

24. What level of interest do you have in participating in a book study where you read a book and then meet once a month to connect with men and comment on what you learned?

Not interested A little interested Somewhat interested Very interested

Men's Conferences

25. What level of interest do you have in going with the men of [Church Name] to attend a one-day conference?

    ☐ Not interested ☐ A little interest ☐ Somewhat interested
    ☐ Very interested

26. How much are you willing to pay for an all day Saturday conference?

    ☐ $20.00 ☐ $40.00 ☐ $60.00 ☐ $80.00 ☐ $100.00

27. What level of interest do you have in going with the men of [Church Name] to attend an overnight conference leaving Friday and returning late Saturday night?

    ☐ Not interested ☐ A little interested ☐ Somewhat interested
    ☐ Very interested

28. How much are you willing to pay for an overnight conference (return home Saturday night)?

    ☐ $40.00 ☐ $60.00 ☐ $80.00 ☐ $100.00 ☐ $120.00

29. What level of interest do you have in going with the men of [Church Name] to attend a full weekend conference leaving Friday and returning home Sunday afternoon?

    ☐ Not interested ☐ A little interested ☐ Somewhat interested
    ☐ Very interested

30. How much are you willing to pay for a full weekend (Friday-Sunday) overnight conference?

   ☐ $80.00   ☐ $100.00   ☐ $120.00   ☐ $140.00   ☐ $160.00

Comments

Thank you for taking the time to help us collect this information. Please share any comments you have on [Name of Men's Ministry] here at [Church Name]

_____

_____

_____

_____

_____

_____

_____

_____

_____

_____

Sample Score Sheet

Demographics								
1. Age		13-19	20-29	30-39	40-49	50-59	60+	
	Totals	1	0	0	0	0	0	
	%	100.00%	0.00%	0.00%	0.00%	0.00%	0.00%	

		Totals	%				
2. Marriage		1	100.00%	Never been married			
		0	0.00%	Was married and am now divorced			
		0	0.00%	Am presently married – first marriage			
		0	0.00%	Am presently married – married more than once			

		Totals	%			
3. Children		1	100.00%	Presently have children living at home under age 13		
		0	0.00%	Presently have children living at home between 13 and 18		
		0	0.00%	Presently have children, who are all living away from home		
		0	0.00%	Presently have no children		

4. How long is your workweek? <40hrs 40-45hrs 46-50hrs 51-55hrs 56-60hrs >60

		<40 hrs	40-45 hrs	45-50 hrs	51-55hrs	55-60 hrs	>60
	Totals	1	0	0	0	0	0
	%	100.00%	0.00%	0.00%	0.00%	0.00%	0.00%

Personal Development

5. How long have you been at your present job

		< 1 yr	2-3 yrs	3-5yrs	6-10 yrs	> 10 yrs
	Totals	1	0	0	0	0
	%	100.00%	0.00%	0.00%	0.00%	0.00%

6. How would you measure your job satisfaction the past twelve months?

		Totals	%	
		1	100.00%	Best year ever in my work life

	0	0.00%	Very satisfying				
	0	0.00%	Satisfying				
	0	0.00%	Less than satisfying				
	0	0.00%	Anxious to move to different employment				

7. How long have you been a Christian?

		< 1 yr	2-3 yrs	3-5yrs	6-10 yrs	> 10 yrs	
	Totals	1	0	0	0	0	
	%	100.00%	0.00%	0.00%	0.00%	0.00%	

8. How would you measure your growth in Christ the last twelve months?

	Totals	%					
	1	100.00%	Most growth ever in my life in Christ				
	0	0.00%	Solid growth—not standing still				
	0	0.00%	Standing still—no measurable growth				
	0	0.00%	Struggling to grow for a variety of reasons				
	0	0.00%	Doing very poorly and need help				

9. Do you have another man who helps you keep accountable in your walk with Christ?

	Totals	%	
	1	100.00%	Yes
	0	0.00%	No

Identify with Christ

10. How often have you invited another man to join you for Sunday morning worship at your church during the past two years?

		Weekly	Monthly	2-3 x yr	Alm Never	Never	
	Totals	1	0	0	0	0	
	%	100.00%	0.00%	0.00%	0.00%	0.00%	

11. How often have you shared the Gospel message with another person during the past two years?

		Weekly	Monthly	2-3 x yr	Alm Never	Never	
	Totals	1	0	0	0	0	

| | % | 100.00% | 0.00% | 0.00% | 0.00% | 0.00% | |

12. If you are married, how often have you invited your wife to pray with you during the last two years (Do not include thanksgiving for meals)?

		Weekly	Monthly	2-3 x yr	Alm Never	Never
	Totals	1	0	0	0	0
	%	100.00%	0.00%	0.00%	0.00%	0.00%

13. If you have children at home, how often in the past two years have you purposely gathered the family together for Bible reading and prayer?

		Weekly	Monthly	2-3 x yr	Alm Never	Never
	Totals	1	0	0	0	0
	%	100.00%	0.00%	0.00%	0.00%	0.00%

Issues Facing Men

14. How often are you exposed to pornography?

		Daily	2-3 week	Weekly	Monthly	2-3 x yr	Never
	Totals	1	0	0	0	0	0
	%	100.00%	0.00%	0.00%	0.00%	0.00%	0.00%

15. How often do you lose your temper?

		Daily	2-3 week	Weekly	Monthly	2-3 x yr	Never
	Totals	1	0	0	0	0	0
	%	100.00%	0.00%	0.00%	0.00%	0.00%	0.00%

16. How often do you gamble (Lottery, casino, on-line)?

		Daily	2-3 week	Weekly	Monthly	2-3 x yr	Never
	Totals	1	0	0	0	0	0
	%	100.00%	0.00%	0.00%	0.00%	0.00%	0.00%

17. How often to you consume alcohol?

		Daily	2-3 week	Weekly	Monthly	2-3 x yr	Never
	Totals	1	0	0	0	0	0
Daily 2-3 Week Weekly Monthly 2-3 times/yr Never	%	100.00%	0.00%	0.00%	0.00%	0.00%	0.00%

18. How much alcohol do you consume (One drink is defined as 12 ounces of beer, 5 ounces of wine, or one standard cocktail (1.5 ounces of 80-proof liquor)?

		Never	Monthly	2-4 x M	2-4 x Wk	>5 Weekly
	Totals	1	0	0	0	0
	%	100.00%	0.00%	0.00%	0.00%	0.00%

19. How many drinks containing alcohol do you have on a typical day when you are drinking?

		1	2-Jan	4-Mar	6-May	>6
	Totals	1	0	0	0	0
	%	100.00%	0.00%	0.00%	0.00%	0.00%

Ministry

20. What kind of Christian small group are you presently involved with (Check all that relate)?

	Totals	%	
	1	100.00%	Not in a regular small group of any kind
	0	0.00%	Once a month small group
	0	0.00%	Weekly or bi-weekly group of men and women
	0	0.00%	Weekly or bi-weekly group of men

21. Are you more likely to:

	Totals	%	
	1	100.00%	Read a Christian book
	0	0.00%	Listen to a Christian CD
	0	0.00%	Listen to Christian radio

| | 0 | 0.00% | Watch a Christian video | | | |
| | 0 | 0.00% | Watch Christian television | | | |

22. Please rate your interest in the items below: 1 = low through 6 = highest (mark one for each item)

Score		1	2	3	4	5	6
a. Men's Bible Study		1	0	0	0	0	0
	%	100.00%	0.00%	0.00%	0.00%	0.00%	0.00%
b. Camping trip		1	0	0	0	0	0
	%	100.00%	0.00%	0.00%	0.00%	0.00%	0.00%
c. Golf scramble		1	0	0	0	0	0
	%	100.00%	0.00%	0.00%	0.00%	0.00%	0.00%
d. Monthly breakfast		1	0	0	0	0	0
	%	100.00%	0.00%	0.00%	0.00%	0.00%	0.00%
e. Chili cook-off		1	0	0	0	0	0
	%	100.00%	0.00%	0.00%	0.00%	0.00%	0.00%
f. Men Sunday school		1	0	0	0	0	0
	%	100.00%	0.00%	0.00%	0.00%	0.00%	0.00%
g. Sporting event		1	0	0	0	0	0
	%	100.00%	0.00%	0.00%	0.00%	0.00%	0.00%
h. Fishing trip		1	0	0	0	0	0
	%	100.00%	0.00%	0.00%	0.00%	0.00%	0.00%
i. Annual retreat		1	0	0	0	0	0
	%	100.00%	0.00%	0.00%	0.00%	0.00%	0.00%
j. Service project		1	0	0	0	0	0
	%	100.00%	0.00%	0.00%	0.00%	0.00%	0.00%
k. Father child outing		1	0	0	0	0	0
	%	100.00%	0.00%	0.00%	0.00%	0.00%	0.00%
l. Equipping seminar		1	0	0	0	0	0
	%	100.00%	0.00%	0.00%	0.00%	0.00%	0.00%

23. If you were to attend a seminar for men in the coming months, which ones would be of interest to you? Please check the top three.

	Totals	%				
	1	100.00%	Furthering my Career			
	0	0.00%	Godly Fathering			

152

		0	0.00%	Lust/Sexual Temptation			
		0	0.00%	Time Management			
		0	0.00%	Rites of Passage Training			
		0	0.00%	Discipleship/Spiritual Growth			
		0	0.00%	Developing a Friendship with my wife			
		0	0.00%	Deepening my Marriage			
		0	0.00%	Becoming a Great Dad			
		0	0.00%	Managing money/Budgets			
		0	0.00%	Dealing with Anger			
		0	0.00%	Other _____			

24. What level of interest do you have in participating in a book study where you read a book and then meet once a month to connect with men and comment on what you learned?

	No interest	A little interested	Somewhat Interested	Very Interested
Totals	1	0	0	0
%	100.00%	0.00%	0.00%	0.00%

Men's Conferences

25. What level of interest do you have in attending a one-day conference?

	No interest	A little interested	Somewhat Interested	Very Interested
Totals	1	0	0	0
%	100.00%	0.00%	0.00%	0.00%

26. How much are you willing to pay for an all day Saturday conference?

	$20.00	$40.00	$60.00	$80.00	$100.00
Totals	1	0	0	0	0
%	100.00%	0.00%	0.00%	0.00%	0.00%

27. What level of interest do you have in attending an overnight conference leaving Friday and returning late Saturday night?

	No interest	A little interested	Somewhat Interested	Very Interested
Totals	1	0	0	0
%	100.00%	0.00%	0.00%	0.00%

28. How much are you willing to pay for an overnight conference (return home Saturday night)?

	$20.00	$40.00	$60.00	$80.00	$100.00

153

Totals	1	0	0	0	0
%	100.00%	0.00%	0.00%	0.00%	0.00%

29. What level of interest do you have in attending a weekend conference leaving Friday and returning home Sunday afternoon?

	No interest	A little interested	Somewhat Interested	Very Interested
Totals	1	0	0	0
%	100.00%	0.00%	0.00%	0.00%

30. How much are you willing to pay for a full weekend (Friday – Sunday) overnight conference?

	$40.00	$60.00	$80.00	$100.00	>$120.00
Totals	1	0	0	0	0
%	100.00%	0.00%	0.00%	0.00%	0.00%

ABOUT THE AUTHORS

BRIAN DOYLE

Brian Doyle serves as Founder, CEO, and President of Iron Sharpens Iron which equips churches to train men for spiritual leadership. He oversees the ISI Network which hosts equipping conferences for men around the nation. He also serves on the National Coalition of Ministries to Men and The Fatherhood Commission. Brian and his wife, Barb, have five children.

BRAD STEWART

Dr. Brad Stewart is a men's ministry leader, disciple maker, author, and passionate man of God. He currently serves as President of Kingdom Warrior Ministries, is a retired US Navy Senior Chief Petty Officer and fellow Navigator. In addition, Brad serves as an advisory member on the Columbia Evangelical Seminary board or regents. He and his wife reside in Sedro-Woolley, WA.

RON R. FRASER

Ron Fraser, MBA, M.Div, Ph.D. President and CEO of PointMan Ministries; Licensed Minister, Pastoral Counselor, Leadership Coach and Ministry consultant. He devotes much of his time to helping local and national pastors and church leaders "Win with Their Men," through Biblically based teaching and training seminars using the PointMan Ministries curriculum he is helping to develop, and as well as the Iron Sharpens Iron curriculum and resources.

TOM CHESHIRE

Tom Cheshire serves as Founder and Executive Director of Relevant Practical Ministry for Men, which exists to be a resource to the local church specifically in the area of men's discipleship. He is also a charter member of the national ministry, Iron Sharpens Iron, and hosts four national equipping conferences in the Midwest. He serves as an elder in his local church with overseeing discipleship as well as other areas of responsibility. Tom is married to Jan and they have two adult daughters.

DAVE ENSLOW
Dave Enslow is the founder and director of Next Steps for Men, a regional ministry in Florida serving the local church, to help train and equip men to effectively disciple others. Dave believes that spiritual growth for men will occur best in the context of small groups connected with the local church, "because, when you build into men, everyone will benefit."

ENDNOTES

1 http://www.ccel.org/ccel/bruce/twelve.v.html

2 See NMLB ch. 8

3 *Readers Digest*, January, 1992

4 Men's Ministry in the 21st Century (Loveland, CO. Group Publishing, 2004) pg. 86

CPSIA information can be obtained
at www.ICGtesting.com
Printed in the USA
FSOW03n0007090217
30534FS